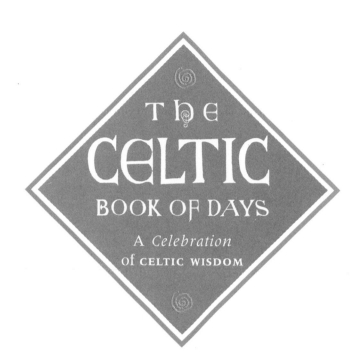

The
CELTIC
BOOK OF DAYS

A *Celebration*
of CELTIC WISDOM

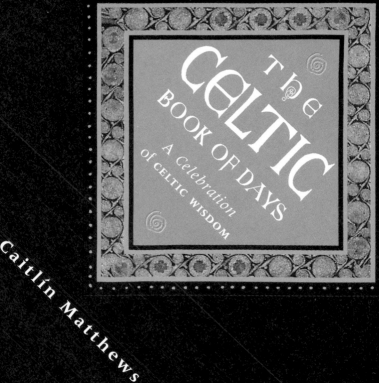

The CELTIC BOOK OF DAYS

A Celebration of Celtic Wisdom

Caitlín Matthews

Published in Ireland by
Gill & Macmillan Ltd
Goldenbridge
Dublin 8
with associated companies throughout the world

Copyright © 1995 *Godsfield Press Ltd*
Text © 1995 *Caitlín Matthews*
Illustrations © 1995 *Amanda Cameron*

Designed by
The Bridgewater Book Company Ltd
Kate Overy/Peter Bridgewater
Picture research by *Vanessa Fletcher*
Mac Artist *John Fowler*

ISBN 0–7171–2326–X

A CIP catalogue record for this book is
available from the British Library

Printed in Singapore

DEDICATION

To Maggie Connolly

and to all who celebrate the
year's turning with joy

Sínim mo phenn mbec mbraenach
tar aenach lebar lígoll
cen scor fri selba ségonn.

I send my poor pen over an
assembly of beautiful books without
cease for the heritage of the
distinguished company.

CONTENTS

The Gates of the Year

AS WE APPROACH THE THIRD MILLENNIUM, a great spiritual hunger to recapture the lore, traditions and wisdom of our ancestors is rising in the West. This search is not merely fuelled by a nostalgia for past times, before the intervention of the agricultural and industrial revolutions, nor by an atavistic yearning for past political power and greatness. Throughout the western world and its farthest flung colonies, there is a deep hunger to re-appreciate ancestral heritage in a contemporary context, to live lives of greater spiritual meaning and planetary integration. Since the customs and traditions of the Celtic world are integrated into the elements and seasons in a way which few western traditions now enjoy, it is to the Celtic tradition that many have turned as part of their quest. Indeed, many have adopted the Celtic calendar and its seasonal celebrations as a means of personal and spiritual discovery.

The way in which we observe and celebrate the unfolding year is very important to our daily life. This is especially true when the majority of us live in an urban environment where the seasonal shifts are less readily perceptible, where the growth cycle which annually unfolds is much easier to ignore.

As human beings, we are also part of the growth cycle of the planet, being nourished by the elements, by vegetation and animal life and, at the end of our cycle, in turn providing nourishment for those same elements, vegetation and animal life. As year succeeds year, each season provides new lessons, insights and opportunities for us to understand our role in the planetary web of life. One way of becoming more consciously aware and reconnected with this web of life is to celebrate the seasonal round and look for the opening of the magical gates of the year as day succeeds day.

This book is an attempt to trigger such opportunities, to help the gates of the year to become more manifest: as you read each entry, it is also good to become more aware of the season through which you are passing and the possibilities which daily arise.

The arrangement of this book is according to Celtic custom, by which the year is divided into four periods, each heralded by a quarterly festival:

Samhain	the Winter quarter of *November, December, January*;
Imbolc	the Spring quarter of *February, March, April*;
Beltane	the Summer quarter of *May, June, July*;
Lughnasadh	the Autumn quarter of *August, September, October*.

Each of the Celtic festivals is a gateway, marking the four periods which correspond to the growth cycle of rest, sprouting, burgeoning and fruiting. It may seem strange to have a calendar which starts in November, but these festival gateways were historically designated by the lunar cycle which underlies the agricultural year which ends and begins in the late Autumn when harvest is over and the soil is prepared for Winter planting.

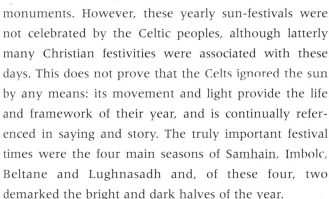

THE CELTIC YEAR

This diagram shows the Celtic year and the ways in which the four seasons are heralded through the gateways of the Celtic festivals. Each season has a month of preparation, manifestation and exposition.

The Solstices and Equinoxes mark the movement of the sun: this progress was visible to most ancient peoples and is often reflected in the erection and orientation of many megalithic monuments. However, these yearly sun-festivals were not celebrated by the Celtic peoples, although latterly many Christian festivities were associated with these days. This does not prove that the Celts ignored the sun by any means: its movement and light provide the life and framework of their year, and is continually referenced in saying and story. The truly important festival times were the four main seasons of Samhain, Imbolc, Beltane and Lughnasadh and, of these four, two demarked the bright and dark halves of the year.

Samhain marked the beginning of Winter and also of the dark half; Beltane marked the beginning of Summer and the light half. Why these two dates? The rising of the Pleiades occurs at the time of Samhain: they set at the time of Beltane. For a mobile people such as the Celts, the major seasonal festivals were first codified in the days

of their wandering migration across Europe and were therefore observed by the movement of the stars.

There is undoubtedly much more Celtic star lore which we have lost. Pliny wrote that the druids reckoned months, years and ages by the moon, and this is borne out by the Gaulish calendrical tablet found at Coligny in France, as well as by the common Celtic expression of 'a nine-night' as a unit of time. It has been suggested that the Celts may have had a twenty-seven day month made up of three such nine-nights. We do know, however, that each twenty-four hour period began at sunset among the Celts, with nights preceding days: this also testifies to the importance of moon and star-rising among them as indicators of the quarterly festivals.

In this book, the Celtic festivals have been designated on calendrical dates, however it seems evident from the internal evidence of texts and customs that the four Celtic festivals would have been celebrated on the full moon: thus, Samhain would have been celebrated on the first full moon of the winter season, not necessarily on the evening of 31st October. The Celtic year was therefore much more flexible than our modern calendar. I have not sought to integrate the two, since, to be strictly accurate and reflect Celtic custom, this book would need to be linked to the nineteen-year circuit of the moon, with each year having its own lunar pattern.

Each of the four seasons has its own traditional characteristics which I have striven to bring out in the selection of material. Samhain is the period for ancestral communion and introspection; Imbolc is associated with beginnings and primal innocence; Beltane is a period for creative and powerful expression; Lughnasadh is associated with maturity and consolidation.

Each calendar day of the year has its own entry, drawn from a variety of material. Included are natural features such as lakes and rivers, wells, forests, islands; heroic, mythic and saintly folk appear, as do the people of the gift – the poets, druids and musicians of old. The saints are commemorated on their own feast day. Characters from stories and deities from Celtic myth are accorded days most suited to the nature of their legend. There are selections from bardic lore and poetry, stories, weather and faery lore, customs, celebrations, animal wisdom, prophecies and riddles.

Because the integration of personal spirituality into daily life is a strong feature of Celtic tradition, I have included many prayers, blessings and invocations from both primal and Christian streams of Celtic spirituality;

each stream has its own wisdom, neither is 'better' nor 'more holy' than the other. In Celtic tradition, the soul is mobile, ardent and true: like the many-tracked strands of Celtic interlacing and knotwork, the soul is faithful to its own nature and pathway.

The material in this book is from insular rather than continental Celtic sources, from many eras of Celtic people, from primal through to Christian belief, from the ranks of ordinary and privileged people, from customs celebrated in ancient and in modern times. In drawing upon a network of such vastly disparate times, places and criteria my intention has been to stress the enduring nature of the Celtic peoples rather than to weave a false or idealized tapestry.

Each entry within this book is but one thread in a much wider web which is still being woven, for this is the true meaning of tradition: a transmission of knowledge which is being continually updated and practised in new and more appropriate ways in every generation. No custom or piece of wisdom endures in a vacuum: it is influenced by the people who live within that culture.

The factors which connect us with our Celtic ancestors are the lands upon which they lived, that gives us our sense of place; the traditions that they practised, which give us our sense of space; and the seasons that connect us both through many layers of time. For many people reading this book in other parts of the world, only the sense of space and time will be relevant, for they inhabit a different place that has its own wisdom.

The Celtic people who live around the world are no less Celtic than their brothers and sisters who still live in the Celtic homelands; but it is plain that new homelands and local customs will influence seasonal celebrations to a greater degree, especially when one lives in the southern hemisphere, for example.

Traditions cannot be preciously preserved unaltered, yet we can still commemorate and celebrate our ancestral heritage with respect in whatever lands we inhabit, as well as acknowledging the spirit of place with the same awe and sense of discovery as our Celtic ancestors, who were themselves incomers to new lands. Wherever they roam, the Celtic peoples exercise their subtle, elusive and enriching imagination, testifying to the strength of the ancestral myths and customs. To them and their descendants, I wish a long and happy life and the triple blessing of memory, truth and respect.

May the year turn blessedly for you, and may the gates of the year reveal new treasures in every season of your life!

9

CAITLÍN MATTHEWS
Twelfth Night 1995

NOTES
Sources of quotations are referenced by name to the bibliography (p.125–6)
Entries followed by (CM) indicate original translations specially made by the author for this book

SAMHAIN

IN WINTER'S GRIP

Samhain marks the Celtic New Year as the Winter season begins. This may seem a strange season to begin the new year, but, as the days draw darker, shorter and colder, as the trees become bare and leafless, the agricultural year is at its close and its beginning. The growth cycle begins in the darkest depths of Winter when the cold forces seeds to germinate in preparation for their Spring emergence. Although all seems dead, life rests and waits for the returning light. The period of Samhain is a good time for introspection, giving space for personal perspective and reflection.

The Faery Raid

1

THE FESTIVAL OF SAMHAIN began the winter half of the year. It was believed that the Cailleach, the aspect of the Goddess who appeared as an old woman, hit the ground with her hammer, making it iron hard until Imbolc. On Samhain night, the gates of the otherworld were open, allowing communion with the ancestors. In the Christian era, the festival was reassigned to the Feast of All Saints however, many of the customs surrounding modern Hallowe'en (the Eve of All Hallows or Saints) still concern this ancient understanding of the accessibility of the dead at this time. The ancestors were respected as the repositories of lore and wisdom: many Celtic tales speak of the dead returning to speak to their descendants in order to impart knowledge or to restore memory of ancient customs and stories. The feasts of both Samhain and Beltane were considered to be outside the boundaries of normal activities, when supernatural events take place: the barriers between humans, ancestors, gods and faeries are overthrown, and they can visit each others' realms. The modern festival of Hallowe'en, All Saints Eve, derives from the ancient Celtic festival of Samhain, called Nos Cyn Calan Gauaf in Welsh.

2

THE CUSTOM OF SOUL-CAKING, where children go round the village to beg for cakes in return for praying for the souls of the departed was still done in Cheshire up to the 19th century; this was a vestige of the Feast of All Souls when prayers for the dead were said, and, more anciently, of the respect and remembrance of the ancestors. A mumming or souling play still circulates Antrobus, Cheshire, accompanied by a hobby horse. This horse is one of many which circulate several regions of Britain and Ireland during the winter months, a distant reminder of the winter mare aspect of the Cailleach.

3

ST GWENFREWI OR WINEFRIDE (6TH CENTURY) lived at Treffynon or Holywell in Clwyd where she was courted by prince Caradoc, whom she repulsed. In his rage, he struck off her head and where it fell to the ground, a fountain sprang up. Her uncle, St Beuno restored her to life and she lived on as abbess to a nunnery at Holywell. It became a place of pilgrimage where people bathed in the waters of the fountain for various cures in the early Middle Ages, and is still visited today. 'The bright water bubbles forth, sweet fountain against critical illness.'

(HENKEN)

13

NOVEMBER

4

MOVING TUATHAL OR WIDDERSHINS, against the sun, was avoided by all Celtic people, lest it bring bad luck. Walking, stirring things *deosil* (*see 2nd May*) maintained the natural order; to walk *tuathal* was to begin a journey badly. *Tuathal* derives from 'to move left'.

NOVEMBER

5

THROUGHOUT THE CELTIC WORLD, the wealth of the oral tradition was maintained by triadic sayings which were memorized by bards and poets to be uttered at appropriate moments. Often these triads encapsulated complex stories but often, as with the one that follows, the triads spoke of the common wisdom of life. Three things heralding trouble: holding plough-land in common; performing feats together; alliance in marriage.

NOVEMBER

6

ST ILLTUD (D. EARLY 6TH CENTURY), founder of the abbey of Llantwit Major, studied with St Germanus of Auxerre. He is said to have been a cousin of King Arthur's and become one of his warriors, but to have put aside arms and taken orders. In his Wonders of Britain, the ninth century chronicler, Nennius, describes how St Illtud was praying at Llwynarth on the Gower Peninsula, when he received the body of a holy man for secret burial, 'lest men swear by it'; over the corpse, an altar miraculously hung, remaining in the air despite being tested by a man who thrust a rod beneath it. The identity of the corpse some speculate to be the body of Arthur himself. Illtud's bell is credited with protecting the people of Wales.

NOVEMBER

7

THE CELTS RECKONED each twenty-four hour interval from nightfall followed by day, so that the fall of night betokened the new 'day'. The reckoning of feast-days is thus from twilight, not from dawn. Julius Caesar wrote of the Celts: 'in reckoning birthdays and the new moon and the near year their unit of reckoning is the night followed by the day'. (ELLIS)

NOVEMBER

8

THE NUMBER TWENTY-SEVEN appears frequently in Celtic lore, since it is composed of three nines, a threefold tripling of the sacred number nine. There are traces of a nine night week in ancient tradition, perhaps making up a lunar month of twenty-seven nights. War-bands and royal retinues were often composed of twenty-seven people, making twenty-eight with the chieftain or war-leader.

9

Lyn tegid, at Bala, is the largest natural lake in Wales. It is the home of Ceridwen, the initiator of the Welsh poet, Taliesin.

10

Arawn, god of annwn, the Welsh Underworld is the leader of the Wild Hunt which, with its pack of white hounds with red-tipped ears, is heard baying through winter skies. To Pwyll of Dyfed he granted the hospitality of Annwn, gifting him with the very first pigs. Arawn is patron of all who have no means of just vindication.

11

Martinmas is named for the Gaulish St Martin, Bishop of Tours (316–397). Born in Hungary, Martin became a Roman soldier, but as a catechumen he found his Christian faith at odds with his occupation, whereupon he became a conscientious objector. After discharge from the army, he became a pioneer of Western monasticism and earned a reputation as a wonder-worker. He unsuccessfully defended the Gnostic sect of Priscillianists from persecution. He is depicted tearing his cloak in half to share with a beggar and his emblem is a globe of fire, which was said to be seen over his head when saying Mass, and a goose, whose migration usually coincides with his feast. On this day, surplus animals which could not be over-wintered in barns through lack of fodder and shelter, were traditionally slaughtered and salted down for winter eating.

12

The pre-roman celtic sanctuary at Roquepertuse in Provence, was entered through a trilithon stone portal in which were carved niches for human heads. For the Celts, the seat of the soul was the head: these heads may have been those of fallen enemies, to be offered to the gods of the shrine. The genius of Roquepertuse seems to have been depicted in the form of a goose or bird of prey. Within insular Celtic tradition, the raven holds the same function: this bird is associated with the Goddess of War, the Morrighan.

13

The death-watch was a Celtic method of divination still upheld in the West of England until the last century: to watch in the church porch at midnight, usually during Midsummer, New Year's Eve or Hallow'een, to see the apparitions of those who would die in the parish in the next year.

15

14

SCATHACH, THE EPONYMOUS GODDESS of the Island of Skye, was the martial teacher of Cuchulainn and other heroes. The role of warrior woman and combat-tutor was a feature of Celtic martial education. She is the matron of self-defence and female independence, as well as the guardian of young people who seek to know their full potential.

15

THIS SCOTS GAELIC BLESSING invokes the angels to guard our sleep:

May the angels watch me
As I lie down to sleep.
May angels guard me
As I sleep alone.

Uriel be at my feet,
Ariel be at my back,
Gabriel be at my head,
Raphael be at my side.

Michael protect my soul
With the strong shield of love.
And the healing Son of Mary
Touch my eyes with blessedness.

16

TLACHTGA, GODDESS of the thunderbolt-spear, was daughter to the druid, Mog Ruith. She created the pillar-stone of Cnamchaill which killed all who touched it, blinded those who saw it and deafened those who heard it. She gave her name to the Hill of Ward, near Athboy in Co. Meath, which is where the ceremonial Samhain fires were kindled. She is the matron of hidden knowledge and all those who receive sudden revelation.

17

One of the Three Powerful Swineherds of Britain was Coll ap Collfrewy who guarded the sow, Henwen. In British myth, she is said to have brought forth a grain of wheat and a bee in Gwent, a grain of barley and a bee in Pembroke, a wolf-cub and an eagle in Snowdonia, and a fearsome kitten, called Palug's Cat, in Arfon, which only Cei, warrior of Arthur was able to subdue.

S<small>T HILDA</small> (614–680), was an Anglo-Saxon noblewoman who founded the double monastery of Whitby and was the hostess of the Synod of Whitby, a council held to bring harmony between Celtic and Roman usages of the Church. Raised in Celtic Christianity and a protegéc of St Aidan, she supported Colman who spoke for the Celtic usage. She encouraged Caedman, a lay-brother who had miraculously been given the gift of song, in turning scripture into vernacular song.

L<small>INDOW MAN</small>, facetiously nick-named 'Pete Moss', was discovered as a peat-preserved body in the Lindow Moss in Cheshire in 1984. Extensive forensic and archaeological examination show him to have suffered the ritual 'three-fold death', having been pole-axed, garotted and his throat cut in about 4th century BC. Sacrificial bog-bodies of a comparable kind have been found in Denmark, and the nature of Lindow Man's threefold death is borne out in textual evidence of Celtic myth. The body is currently exhibited in the British Museum, London.

S<small>AMHAIN IS TRADITIONALLY</small> the quarter when the elders and ancestors are honoured and remembered. In many parts of the Celtic world, the ancestors and the faeries are one and the same. Scrupulous observance of faery pathways, dancing and gathering places is still upheld in Celtic lands by those who wish to stay in good relations with the unseen inhabitants of the otherworld who live about us. It is considered the height of bad manners to build houses on such pathways or to remove faery trees such as hawthorns.

ST COLUMBANUS (543–615) was an Irish missionary to Europe with a monastery in Bobbio. He maintained the Celtic, not Roman, rule and wrote to Pope Boniface IV to proclaim the fact that 'we Irish, inhabitants of the world's edge ... are disciples of those who write the sacred canon inspired by the Holy Spirit.' He admonished the Pope roundly with 'for among us it is not who you are but how you make your case that counts,' drawing upon the druidic method of disputation. (O'FIACH)

18

A GAULISH CALENDRICAL TABLET made of bronze was found in Coligny in 1897. Dated to the first century AD it depicts a complex collation of meteorological information to form a series of lunar months, making up a thirty-year system comprising five cycles of sixty-two lunation sets with one sixty-one lunation to complete it. It shows lucky and unlucky days and gives Gaulish names for the lunar months. The month of October-November is called Samonios or Seed-Fall, referring to the falling nuts and seed-cases of Autumn.

THIS IRISH POEM laconically evokes the stark beginning of Winter :

My tidings for you: the stag bells,
Winter snows, summer is gone.

Wind high and cold, low the sun,
Short his course, sea running high.

Deep-red the bracken, its shape all gone –
The wild goose has raised his wonted cry.

Cold has caught the wings of birds:
Season of ice – these are my tidings.

TRANS. MEYER

ALL IRISH LETTERS of the ogham alphabet are tree-names. Ogham was a method of straight-line inscription which bisected the edge of a stone or stave of wood. Many Irish texts speak of 'ogham libraries' or wisdom being preserved by some manner of encryption, decipherable only by poets and druids. The writing of short messages or prophetic devices upon four-sided wooden staves was a common method of communication over distance. In the Irish tree alphabet, the letter A is represented by ailm, or scots pine tree.

REPRESENTATIONS of three figures in long hooded cloaks are found throughout Celto-Roman Britain; they are called the Three Hooded Ones or the *Genii Cucullati*, from *cucullus* – a hood. They nearly always accompany depictions of Celtic goddesses of plenty and may be the earliest representations of the faery folk as spirits of the place.

COVENTINA WAS THE GODDESS of the spring at Carrawburgh, called by the Romans, Brocolita, near Hadrian's Wall. She is depicted reclining on a leaf, with a water-lily leaf in her hand, or else, in company with two other water-nymphs, who pour water from a beaker. Dedications to her have been discovered throughout Western Europe. Hers is one of the few representations of a well-goddess, and her cult seems to have been upheld by many women who left offerings of pins in the spring.

ST VIRGIL OR FERGHIL (D.784) was an Irish monk who won favour at the court of Pippin the Short. He became Abbot of St Peters, Salzberg. St Boniface took severe exception to Virgil's appointment and brought him to the attention of Pope Zachiarias, who said he would endanger his own soul if Virgil persisted in teaching the existence of another world below our own with its own sun and moon. Many believe that Virgil was promoting the faery realms of his native Ireland. He is one of the rare few Celtic saints to have been formally canonized.

20

NOVEMBER
28

S T CANAIR (D.530) built a cell near Bantry Bay, Co. Cork. She had a vision of all the churches of Ireland glowing with light. The strongest light issued from nearby Scattery Island when St Senan lived, so Canair went to learn from him. Senan, upholding the usual ban upon women staying in the guesthouse, made to send her away. Canair responded, 'Christ came to redeem women no less than to redeem men. He suffered for the sake of women as much as for the sake of men. Women as well as men can enter the heavenly kingdom.' For her persistence Senan granted her hospitality. (SELLNER)

NOVEMBER
29

P ryderi, son of Pwyll, Prince of Dyfed had a spectacular career. At birth, he was stolen from his mother by an otherworldly being, raised as the son of a nobleman and called Gwri Golden-Hair; he was restored to his mother, Rhiannon, who promptly said, 'at last my anxiety is over.' Because of the Celtic custom of naming children from their mother's utterance, the name 'anxiety' or Pryderi stuck. When adult, he was trapped in the otherworld and released by the druidic power of his uncle Manawyddan. He was finally slain by the enchantments of Gwydion of Gwynedd. He is the patron of all who suffer difficulties but overcome them.

NOVEMBER
30

T HE CAILLEACH OR 'VEILED ONE' is the title given to the Goddess in her winter aspect. A caille is a veil, and the title is given also to nuns and as a respectful term to old women or grandmothers. There are a number of cailleachs of different Celtic regions including the Cailleach Beare, the Old Woman of Beare, in South-West Ireland, and the Cailleach Bheur or Blue Hag of Scotland. Her cult is so ancient that only fragments of it exist, telling how she flew through the skies throwing stones out of her apron which fell to earth to become mountain-ranges. She is the 'Old Woman Tossed Up in the Basket' from folk-song, and is associated, in many regions with Mother Carey, who throws down the snows. She is frequently seen as at odds with Brighid, the Goddess associated with Imbolc, but the stories reveal that the Cailleach renews her youth by changing as the seasons succeed each other. In Wales the Cailleach is called the Gwrach.

The Coming of the Green Knight

1

THE DEER'S CRY is the name of a magical invocation ascribed to St Patrick. In this extract, the powers of the elements are invoked:

> I arise today
> Through the strength of heaven:
> Light of sun,
> Radiance of moon,
> Splendour of fire,
> Speed of lightning,
> Swiftness of wind,
> Depth of sea,
> Stability of earth,
> Firmness of rock.

TRANS. MEYER

2

ST MELANGELL (6TH CENTURY) founded a community at Pennant in Montgomerayshire. Legend tells how a hare hunted by Prince Brochfael of Powys took sanctuary in her skirts: he respected both animal and nun and granted the whole valley to her. She remains the matron of small creatures.

3

CU ROI MAC DAIRE, King of Munster, was one of the great judges and challengers of Irish tradition. He appeared in otherworldly guise as a giant to offer a beheading game to the Red Branch Warriors of Ulster: Cu Roi offered his own head to be cut off in exchange for one of the warriors kneeling for a return blow. Only Cuchulainn took up the challenge and was accorded by Cu Roi the accolade of supreme champion of Ireland. This story is a forerunner of the medieval Gawain and the Green Knight story. Cu Roi was eventually betrayed by the complicity of his wife, Blanait with Cuchulainn. So famous was this story that there is a poem in the Welsh *Book of Taliesin* about it:

> The death-song of Corroy
> (Cu Roi) agitates me.
> The betraying warrior,
> rough his temper,
> His evil was greater than
> his renown was great,
> To seize the son of Dayry,
> lord of the southern sea,
> Celebrated was his praise before she (Blanait)
> was entrusted to him.

ED. SKENE

4

THE GOGLEDD OR 'THE OLD NORTH' is the name given to the ancestral territory of the Britons, the modern Welsh people. It covered an area south of Stirling to Loch Lomond, extending over Cumbria, Lancashire and Yorkshire to the Humber estuary. The inhabitants called themselves the Cumbri, from which the name for present day Wales is derived – Cymru. After the Battle of Chester in 615, the Cumbri lost touch with their southern kinsfolk in Wales, retaining for a brief period the kingdoms of Strathclyde, Rheged and the Gododdin.

5

THREE THINGS THAT RUIN WISDOM: ignorance, inaccurate knowledge, forgetfulness. (MEYER)

6

MATH AP MATHONWY was the druidic king of Gwynedd. He is patron of wise judgements.

DECEMBER
7

THE RED BOOK OF HERGEST speaks of winter:

The calends of winter, the time
of pleasant gossiping,
The gale and the storm keep equal pace;
It is the work of the wise to keep a secret.

ED. SKENE

DECEMBER
8

THE NUMBER SEVENTEEN seems to have been associated with the visible new moon. Many stories relate how important conquests or explorations were achieved on this day of the moon. The family of the Tuatha De Danaan were numbered in seventeen triads. The seventeenth generation was considered to mark the limits of ancestral memory which, reckoning three–four generations a century, puts ancestral memory at between four and five hundred years.

DECEMBER
9

THE WELL OF YOUTH is at Loch Ba on the island of Mull, Scotland. It is here that the Cailleach bathed to keep herself ever young. Many legends speak of the Cailleach living to be the mother to generations of peoples and regions.

DECEMBER
10

THE CONSTELLATION of Cassiopeia is called Llys Don, or the Court of Don among the Welsh. Don is the Welsh equivalent of Irish Goddess, Danu, the primal ancestress of the Celtic peoples. The root of their names is discernible in the major rivers of Europe, Danube, Dneister, Don etc. These waterways may well have been the migratory pathways of the Celtic peoples.

DECEMBER
11

MEMORY WAS THE GUARDIAN of all knowledge, which was maintained by oral tradition among the Celts. 'The joint memory of two seniors' or elders telling the teachings from one ear to the next preserved knowledge, the recitation of the poets and bards disseminated it, while the literary tradition of Celtic Christianity finally transcribed it. In druidic tradition, knowledge was not written down – not because the druids were illiterate, since they had knowledge of many ancient languages and communicated in them – but because the transcription of knowledge vitiated the oral primacy of truth.

23

DECEMBER
12

Iₙ ᴛʜᴇ ɪʀɪsʜ ᴛʀᴇᴇ ᴀʟᴘʜᴀʙᴇᴛ, the letter O is represented by oir or the gorse bush.

DECEMBER
13

Tʜᴇ ᴘᴏᴇᴍs of the tenth-century poet, Llywarch Hen, lament the death of his twenty-four sons and his lonely old age:

White are the hilltops; wet the streams;
midnight towers.
Every wise-one draws honour.
I deserve sleep in old age.

Loud are the birds; wet the gravel;
Leaves fall; the shelterless unsouled.
I do not deny that I am ill tonight.

Loud are the birds; wet the shore.
Bright the sky; wide the wave.
Heart withered from longing.

TRANS. CM

DECEMBER
14

Eʟᴇɴ ʟʟᴜᴅᴅᴏɢ, Elen of the Roads, was a princess of Powys who married the Roman Emperor Macsen Wledig (Magnus Maximus); she appeared to him in a dream and he journeyed to Britain to find her. She is credited with the creation of the many highways built at that time. She is the matron of dreams and destinations.

DECEMBER
15

Iₙ ᴛʜᴇ ɢᴀᴜʟɪsʜ ᴄᴀʟᴇɴᴅʀɪᴄᴀʟ ᴛᴀʙʟᴇᴛ, the Coligny Calendar, the month of November-December is called Dumanios or 'The Darkest Depths', as the year turns towards the shortest days and longest nights.

DECEMBER
16

Tᴇɪɴᴍ ʟᴀᴇɢᴅᴀ or 'decoding by means of verse' was one of the Three Illuminations or prophetic skills in which doctors of poetry were expected to be proficient. It involved the trance- like repetition of verse over an unknown object or body which brought clarification and knowledge through shamanic incantation. Accessing knowledge through incantation and poetry is a common feature of Celtic magical tradition.

ST SAMTHANN, abbess of Clonbroney, (D.739) was a generous soul-friend to many, exemplifying a deep and practical spirituality. When asked by a monk whether he should pray sitting, standing or lying, she replied, 'A person should pray in every position.' Similarly, on hearing that a teacher was going abroad the better to serve God, she replied, 'The kingdom of heaven can be reached from every land.'

(SELLNER)

CONCHOBOR MAC NESSA was King of Ulster during the heroic era of the Red Branch Warriors. His rule was temperate and honourable, except for his treatment of Deirdriu and the Sons of Usnech. During an ambush, he received a slingshot made of the brains of his enemy Mac Da Thó in his head. It could not be removed and he was ordered to live a temperate life thereafter. Legend says that on hearing reports of the crucifixion of Christ, he was smitten with rage at the dishonour done to the King of Heaven's son, and rose up to defend him, dying as the sling-shot worked its way into his skull.

EPONA IS A PAN-CELTIC GODDESS to whom inscriptions and dedications are found throughout Europe. She is depicted either riding on a horse or else seated with horses about her or with foals eating from her lap. She was the only Celtic deity officially venerated in Rome, her feast being celebrated on this day between the festivals of Consualia (15 Dec) and Opalia (19 Dec) when the deities of the deep earth were honoured. On this day, draft animals, such as horses, oxen and donkeys were rested. Epona is the matron of the life's circuit from cradle to grave and beyond, often depicted holding the napkin which starts the race and the key which opens the gates of the underworld.

DECEMBER
20

Sᴛ ᴜʀsɪɴᴜs (ᴄ.625) was a companion of St Columbanus. He made his cell in the wilderness of the river Doubs in Switzerland. Bears accompanied him and, later, disciples assembled to found a hospice for the poor.

DECEMBER
21

Mɪᴅᴡɪɴᴛᴇʀ's ᴅᴀʏ is called Alban Arthuan of 'the Light of Arthur' in modern druidism. Midwinter is traditionally reckoned as the birthday of Arthur and the beginning of his fosterage and apprenticeship with Merlin. In the darkest depths of winter, the spark of the new year's light is understood to be rekindled.

DECEMBER
22

Mᴀʀɪᴀɴᴜs sᴄᴏᴛᴜs (ᴄ.1028–82). His Irish name was Maelbrigte, or 'servant of Brighid'. His *Chronicle of the World* outlined the history of the world from creation up till 1082.

DECEMBER
23

Iɴ an Irish text called *The Settling of the Manor of Tara*, the ancient ancestral memory of the long-lived sage, Fintan, is invoked to help restore knowledge to the elders of Ireland. Fintan speaks of the five regions of Ireland and their characteristics. He describes the North of Ireland as traditionally known for: contentions, hardihood, rough places, strifes, haughtiness, unprofitableness, pride, captures, assaults, hardness, wars and conflicts. (*See 22 Mar, 22–3 Jun, 22 Sep*).

DECEMBER
24

Tʜᴇ ʙɪʀᴛʜᴅᴀʏ ᴏꜰ ɪsᴜ ᴍᴀᴄ ᴅᴇ, Jesus son of God, is celebrated in this Gaelic Christmas Carol:

This night is the eve of the great Nativity,
Born is the Son of Mary the Virgin,
The soles of his feet have reached the earth,
The Son of Glory has
come down from on high,
Heaven and earth glow to him,
Joy, let there be joy!

Earth and sphere shine to him,
God the Lord has opened a door;
Son of Mary Virgin, speed to help me,
Christ of hope, Door of health,
Golden sun of hill and mountain,
Joy, let there be joy!

TRANS. CM

25

THIS CORNISH CAROL, *Ma gron war'n gelinen*, jointly celebrates the nativity of Christ and the older veneration of the evergreen as the tree of this season:

> Now the holly bears a berry
>   as white as the milk,
> And Mary bore Jesus,
>   who was wrapped up in silk.
>
> And Mary bore Jesus Christ our
>   Saviour for to be,
> And the first tree in the greenwood,
>   it was the holly.
>
> Now the holly bears a berry as
>   black as the coal,
> And Mary bore Jesus who died
>   for us all.
>
> Now the holly bears a berry
>   as blood is it red,
> Then trust we our Saviour
>   who rose from the dead.

26

THE CUSTOM OF HUNTING THE WREN was once widespread throughout Europe, but was still celebrated in parts of Ireland when the Wren Boys went round the villages with a box on a bier singing this song:

> The wren, the wren,
>   The King of all birds,
> On St Stephen's Day
>   Was caught in the furze.
> And though he is little
>   His family is great;
> So rise up, good people,
>   And give us a treat.

The custom was also performed in Pembrokeshire on Epiphany, when a wooden 'wren-house' was borne about. Nowadays, the Wren Boys, dressed in masks and costumes, rarely carry a dead wren, but an approximation of the traditional bier and still sing their song. This ancient custom reflects the mid-winter lore of the druidic belief in the wren as the most knowledgable of birds: in Gaelic story, it won its title of King of Birds, by flying higher than other birds by perching on an eagle's back.

27

CADAIR IDRIS IS A MOUNTAIN and natural boundary between Gwynedd and Powys. It is said that whoever spends a night alone on the summit will come down mad, blind or a great poet. The summits of many such eminences may well have been used in initiatory bardic and druidic rites as places of power.

28

CLIODNA, AN IRISH GODDESS, lived in Tír Tairngiri, the Land of Promise. She fell in love with the mortal, Ciabhan, and fled with him to Glandore in Co. Cork. While she rested there, the god of the sea and the otherworld, Manannan mac Lir sent a great wave which swept her back to the otherworld. Her three magical birds ate from the apples of the otherworldly tree and uttered such sweet music that the sick could be healed.

29

Guising and mumming plays are celebrated throughout Britain and Ireland at this time of year. An array of archetypal characters include the Fool, the Royal Hero, the Foreign Opponent, the Giant, the Doctor, the He-She and the Wise Man. The play is performed outdoors and goes from village to village; it usually involves the Royal Hero's death and resurrection. In Ireland and Scotland, the players are sometimes known as the Hogmanay Men or Christmas Rhymers.

30

In the irish tree alphabet, the letter U is represented by ur or heather.

31

The eve of new year or Hogmanay is celebrated with greater enthusiasm than Christmas in Scotland, mainly due to the diminution of Christian festivals under Presbyterianism and Calvinism. Toasting the New Year with Het Pint, a bowl of ale spiked with whiskey, the eating of Black Bun or the Hogmanay Bannock and the first-footing of a dark-haired individual carrying fuel and uttering a blessing, were traditionally preceded by the 'redding up' or tidying of the house and its ritual cleansing by brands of smoking juniper. The following blessing was said on Hogmanay in the Western Highlands of Scotland:

The blessing of God upon this house
The blessing of Jesus upon this house
The blessing of the Spirit upon this house
The blessing of Brighid upon this house
The blessing of Michael upon this house
The blessing of Mary upon this house
The blessing of Columba upon this house …
On man and woman, on spouse and child,
on old and young, on maiden and youth.
With plenty of food and plenty of drink,
with plenty of beds and plenty of ale,
with many riches and much cheer,
with many kin and length of life,
Ever upon it.

ED. CARMICHAEL

Morgan le Fay

1

FROM THE IRISH *Colloquy of the Two Sages*, this ritual statement exemplifies the identity of the true Celtic poet:

> I am the child of poetry,
>   Poetry, the child of Reflection,
> Reflection, the child of Meditation,
>   Meditation, the child of Lore,
> Lore, the child of Research,
>   Research, the child of Great Knowledge,
> Great Knowledge, the child of Intelligence,
>   Intelligence, the child of Understanding,
> Understanding, the child of Wisdom,
>   Wisdom, the child of the three gods of Danu.

The three gods of Danu are possibly Brian, Iuchar and Uar, the sons of the Goddess of Inspiration, Brighid; Brighid is frequently associated with the Danaan ancestral Goddess, Danu or Anu, the grandmother of the Tuatha de Danaan.

30

2

THE NORTHERN LIGHTS or the Aurora Borealis were called the Fir-chlisne or Men of the Tricks by the Scottish Gaels, as well as the Merry Dancers: their dance is rarely seen in Southern Britain.

3

DURING THE PERIOD OF SAMHAIN with its long nights, communal entertainment enriched the cold and dark with fresh enchantment. Noson Lawen or 'a merry evening' is the Welsh equivalent of the Gaelic ceilidh, where neighbours assemble at day's end to tell stories and sing songs until the small hours of the morning.

4

GANEIDA, MYRDDIN'S SISTER, is the priestess-sibyl who continues his prophetic work. She creates his otherworldly retreat from which he watches the world. She was conflated, in later medieval tradition, with Nimue, a lady of the lake, who is said to purposely enclose Merlin, having gained his magical secrets. But Ganeida/Nimue is an echo of the ancient Celtic Goddess of the Doorway, who guards the gates of time and occurrence. She appears as the Goddess Ariadne, in Merlin's prophetic vision.

5

THE THREE MOST BEAUTIFUL THINGS in the world: a full-rigged ship, a woman with child and the full moon.

(SHAW)

F AERY LOVERS OF BOTH SEXES who
come to mortal kind are common
in Celtic story. The Faery kind are not
seen as diminutive sprights in Celtic
tradition, but as the immortal and
ancestral spirits who often have communion and conference with human
kind. This *oran sidhe* or faery song
describes the beauty of a faery woman:

I left in the doorway of the bower
  My jewel, the dusky, brown, white-skinned,
Her eye like a star, her lip like a berry,
  Her voice like a stringed instrument.

I left yesterday in the meadow of the kind
  The brown-haired maid of sweetest kiss,
Her eye like a star, her cheek like a rose,
  Her kiss has the taste of pears.

SHAW

T HE NUMBER THIRTY-THREE appears
to be the kingly or judicial number
of honour in Celtic lore. Assemblies of
gods and heroes nearly always number
thirty-two with a chief deity as thirty-
third. Maelduin sails to thirty-two
otherworldly islands and makes his
thirty-third land-fall on his home shore.

I N WALES, Monday is a bad day for
beginning any new project: 'work
begun on Monday will never be a week
old.' Marriages and loans are therefore
avoided on Mondays.

O NE OF THE DEITIES of the Boyne
river in Ireland was Nechtan. He
had a secret well which was also called
the Well of Segais. No-one was allowed
to visit it except for Nechtan and his
three cupbearers. His wife, Boand, went
to investigate the nature of the well for
herself and was overwhelmed by the
waters which flowed out to form a river,
called the Boyne, after Boand.

31

I N THE IRISH TREE ALPHABET, the letter E is represented by edhadh or the aspen. Aspen wood was traditionally used to make the undertaker's measuring rod and was viewed with aversion by Celtic peoples. The tree was later associated with the wood of the cross on which Christ was crucified.

T HIS BLESSING for good health comes from Scots Gaelic tradition; it calls upon the three chief elements of Celtic cosmology – the air, the sea and the land – and their associated animals to disperse the sickness:

> I wish healing upon you,
> The healing of Mary with me,
> Mary, Michael and Brighid
> Be with me all three.
>
> Your pain and sickness
> Be in the earth's depths,
> Be upon the grey stones,
> For they are enduring.
>
> Fly with the birds of the air,
> Fly with the wasps of the hill,
> Swim with the sea-going whale,
> For they are swiftest.
>
> Be upon the clouds of the sky,
> For they are the rainiest,
> Be upon the river's current
> Cascading to the sea.

TRANS. CM

A RIANRHOD IS THE WELSH GODDESS of Destiny and Initiation. Her abode is the otherworldly Caer Sidi, or Spiral Tower, which is a complement of her own name, Silver Wheel; it is identified with the constellation of the Corona Borealis, the Crown of the North. Taliesin speaks of her as a mistress of inspiration.

13

DURING THE SEVENTH CENTURY, Cuirithir the poet came to marry Liadan and found that she had already become a nun; he, in turn, became a monk. This Irish Abelard and Heloise story was fuelled by a continuing love as both lovers submitted to a test of intimacy imposed by St Cummíne of Clonfert, whereby they should occupy the same chamber at night and yet not touch each other. Although eventually parted, their love endured, expressed in some of the finest and bitterest love-poetry, as here in Liadan's lament:

> *Cuirithir the ex-poet loved me;*
> *no benefit to me.*
> *Beloved the lord of the two grey feet:*
> *Sorrow to be without him for eternity.*
> *The stone south of the wooden church*
> *Where the ex-poet stayed,*
> *I visit it at twilight*
> *After the glorious prayer.*
> *He shall have no cow,*
> *Nor no bulling heifer;*
> *No thigh shall rest*
> *Beside the ex-poet's hand.*

TRANS. CM

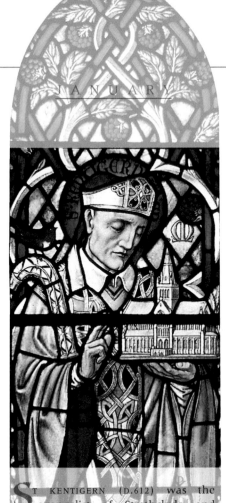

ST KENTIGERN (D.612) was the evangelist of Strathclyde and Cumbria and patron of Glasgow. He was the son of Taneu, a princess of Strathclyde by an unknown father, which caused Taneu and her child to be cast adrift in a coracle. He vindicated the virtue of a queen who had lost her husband's gift, a ring, by extracting it from a salmon. The salmon and ring are still featured in the arms of Glasgow city. Kentigern is also known as Mungo or 'dear one'.

15

ST ITA FOUNDED A MONASTERY at Kileedy, Co. Limerick and died in 570. She had the second sight and was revered as a prophet and healer. She maintained a school for boys and was consequently known as the Foster-mother of the Saints, treating each child as she would the child, Jesus. Her philosophy on childcare may be summed up by her own poem:

> *The fosterage of my house,*
> *is not of any common child;*
> *Jesus with his heavenly company*
> *shelter each night against my heart.*

TRANS. CM

33

IN THE GAULISH CALENDRICAL TABLET, the Coligny Calendar, the month of December-January was called Riuros, 'the Cold Time', when the ice bites deep.

BLATHMAC MAC CÚ BRETTAN was an 8th-century Irish monk who wrote a poetic version of the *Gnostic Gospel of Thomas*, and other religious poems. Here he speaks of Christ:

> *He is the overlord of every generation,*
> *He is the tip of the true vine,*
> *He is the brightly-lit pathway,*
> *He is the true door to the eternal land.*
>
> TRANS. CM

THE LUIDEAG OR WASHER at the ford was an apparition which most warriors wished never to meet as she was encountered on the eve of battle, washing out the bloody shirts of those to be slain the next day. Although she was feared, her action was a kindly one for, as an aspect of the Cailleach, she washed out the blood of one life into the river, making the garment of flesh white once again ready to assume a new life.

THE TARBH-FEIS OR BULL PROPHECY was performed when druids sought out the help of spirits. A bull was slaughtered and its hide removed; the druid lay down on a bed of rowan-wattles, wrapping round him the bullshide, bloody side next to him. Dreams and visions that were observed during his sleep or trance brought the prophetic knowledge that was sought.

IN THE IRISH TREE ALPHABET, the letter I is represented by iodha or yew, the longest lived of all trees. Recent research by Alan Meredith has proved that some churchyard yews, especially those on the north side of churches, are of Celtic antiquity: this is due to the early Church's practice of siting foundations on old pagan ones. (MILNER)

THE ANAM-CHARA OR SOUL-FRIEND IS an important factor in the spiritual health of Celtic Christianity. A soul-friend was the confidant and spiritual advisor, not necessarily a priest and often a lay-person. St Brigit of Kildare said that 'anyone without a soul-friend is like a body without a head.'

AVALON, THE ISLAND OF APPLES, is the otherworldly realm to which King Arthur is ferried, there to be healed of his last wound. The mistress of the island is Morgen, the Healing Goddess who later came to be known as Morgan le Fay in medieval legend.

BANBA IS ONE of the ancient goddesses of Ireland, the wife of Mac Cuill. Her name has become synonymous with the land of Ireland as a poetic metaphor.

JANUARY
24

Twrch trwyth was a ferocious otherworldly boar hunted by King Arthur and his men in fulfillment of the mission of Culhwch to obtain the sacred comb and shears which lay between the ears of the boar; these were to barber the giant Ysbaddaden Pencawr for the marriage of his daughter, Olwen, to Culhwch and were a condition of the match. The boar eventually is chased into the sea and the power of Ysbaddaden is overthrown as soon as his hair is shaved off, leaving Culhwch to marry Olwen.

JANUARY
25

St dwynwen, (5th–6th century) the matron of lovers and all types of friendship, was the daughter of Brychan Brycheiniog. Caught between the love of Prince Maelon and a marriage to another prince, she prayed to be cured of love. Angelic intervention restored her friendship with Maelon after she became a nun. Her symbol is the bow of destiny, the crescent new moon. Her festivities included the making of love spells and the giving of love tokens between sweethearts. She grants faithful lovers union or enables them to forget each other. In Wales this day is more important than St Valentine's day.

JANUARY
26

Cernunnos, the antler-crowned God of the Wild, was venerated throughout the Indo-European world. A depiction of him upon the Gundestrup Cauldron shows him cross-legged, holding a ram-headed serpent. He is the Master of the Animals and a threshold guardian for those seeking fertility, regeneration and initiation into the Celtic mysteries.

JANUARY
27

Three people that are hardest to talk to: a king bent on conquest, a Viking in his armour, and a low-born man protected by patronage.

JANUARY
28

The british god, Nodens, is the Celtic God of Dreams and Visions. He is cognate with Nudd, Lludd Llaw Ereint and the Irish Nuadu of the Silver Hand, and had a temple at Lydney on the banks of the Severn which, on excavation, proved to have a series of abatons or dream-incubatory chambers. Seeking divination or knowledge through dreaming is common among many peoples who have a rich oral tradition, such as the Celts.

JANUARY
29

ᵍILDAS THE WISE (495–570) was of Pictish stock and educated in Brittany. He is chiefly known as the author of the vituperative and uncomplimentary chronicles called *The Wasting of Britain*, a searing polemic against civil and military rulers which sees even the Battle of Badon, at which King Arthur overcame the Saxons, as the act of an unnamed usurper. His failure to mention the author of this signal victory can be put down to the fact that Arthur may have been instrumental in the slaying of Gildas' kinsman, Cuill (Hueil): 'and after the murder, Arthur went home, very pleased to have killed his strongest enemy.'

JANUARY
30

ᵀHIS SCOTS GRACE is traditionally said on Burns Night, 25 January:

Some hae meat that canna eat,
And some wad eat that want it;
But we hae meat and we can eat,
Sae let the Lord be thankit.

And is concluded by:

O Lord, since we hae feasted thus,
Whilk we sae little merit,
Let Meg noo tak awa the flesh,
And Jock bring in the spirit.

JANUARY
31

ᵀHE EVE OF IMBOLC sees the Cailleach's farewell. This is part of the long poem attributed to the Cailleach Beare:

Ebbtide to me as of the sea!
Old age causes me reproach …
I am the old Woman of Beare,
An ever-new smock I used to wear:
Today – such is my mean estate –
I wear not even a cast-off smock …
O happy the isle of the great sea
Which the flood reaches after the ebb!
As for me, I do not expect
Flood after ebb to come to me.
TRANS. MEYER

The festival of Imbolc is now ready to begin and Brighid stands waiting to be welcomed in.

IMBOLC

SPRING'S APPROACH

As the light lengthens, so the cold strengthens,' goes the old saying. The stark coldness of February seems winter-locked until we see the emerging tips of snowdrops to herald the return of Spring. As the lengthening shafts of sunlight pierce the earth, all growing things puts forth shoots, buds begin to open and flowers bloom in great variety. The season of Imbolc encompasses the sprouting period of young growth when we emerge from the introspection of Winter to the fresh hope of each new Spring.

St Brighid, Foster-mother of the Gael

IMBOLC HERALDS the opening of the second quarter of the year. This season is under the aegis of the Irish Goddess Brighid; she is of the Tuatha de Danaan and inherits the mantle of Danu, the ancestress of the Celtic people. Brighid has three aspects, being a matron of healing, smithcraft and poetry; she is lauded by the gifted people – the poets – as the mistress of inspiration and prophecy. Her primacy within Britain and Ireland is marked by many springs, wells and rivers dedicated to her. She has resonances with Brigantia, the territorial Goddess of Northern Britain.

This festival coincides with the birth of lambs and the lactation of ewes, which underlies the meaning of the word, Imbolc. Many aspects of the Irish Goddess's cult became subsumed in that of St Brigit of Kildare (450–523) who was fostered in a druidic household and founded a monastery at Kildare, which maintained a perpetual sacred fire, tended by nineteen nuns. This fire burned from the 5th century and was not extinguished until the Reformation, when all monastic foundations were dissolved. The fiery connections of Brighid/Brigit are still maintained in parts of the Gaelic world whenever the fire is raised in the morning or smoored (covered) at night, by invocatory prayers. St Brigit is known in Wales as St Ffraid and in Scotland as St Bride,

and so is venerated in all parts of the insular Celtic world. Brighid/Brigit is one of the most important bridging figures between Pagan and Christian Celtic traditions, acting as foster-mother to Christ in many legends. In Ireland, she is called 'the Mary of the Gael' and her protective mantle is invoked as a palladium against all dangers. Her rites are still celebrated at Imbolc by the making of Brigit's Crosses out of interwoven rushes which are hung near the door of house, barn and stable. St Brigit is the secondary saintly protector of Ireland, after Patrick.

As the Cailleach had hardened the earth with her hammer at the beginning of Samhain, so Brighid was believed to make it soft again with her white wand, with which she awoke growth, as the following chant makes clear:

Bride dipped her finger in the river
On the Feast day of Bride,
And away went the hatching
mother of the cold;
She washed the palms of her
hands in the river
On the Feast Day of Patrick,
And away went the conceiving
mother of the cold.

ED. JONES

41

THE CHRISTIAN FESTIVAL of Candlemas celebrates the coming of Mary into the Temple, according to the Jewish laws of purification. The Eastern Orthodox world celebrated this feast from the 6th century and it was later adopted by the Western Church. Candles are brought into church and blessed to celebrate the epiphany of the sacred light. Legend tells how St Brigit was instrumental in helping the Holy Family escape from the depredations of Herod's soldiers. As Mary, Jesus and Joseph were passing by on their way into Egypt, Herod's soldiers came into view: Brigit speedily made a crown of candles and capered ecstatically to attract the soldiers' attention. This day was officially the end of the Christmas season when all greenery and decorations were to be taken down.

3

THIS GAELIC LULLABY invokes differ-ent birds in their habitat to soothe a child to sleep:

> The nest of the curlew
>   Is in the bubbling peat-moss,
> My little one will sleep and
>   he shall have the bird.
>
> The nest of the oyster-catcher
>   Is among the smooth shingles,
> My little one will sleep and
>   he shall have the bird.
>
> The nest of the heron
>   Is in the pointed trees,
> My little one will sleep and
>   he shall have the bird.

ED. CARMICHAEL

42

4

IN THE IRISH TREE ALPHABET, the letter B is represented by beith or birch. This tree, which stands as the first letter of the ogham alphabet, is also the first tree to emerge from the glacial ice when vegetation grows after an Ice Age.

5

THREE THINGS that should not be despised: a ragged young man, a shaggy filly and a freckle-legged girl.

6

THIS CHARM for attracting a straying animal comes from Western Scotland:

> I say this rune in your right ear
>   For your good and not for your harm.
> Love of the land that is under your foot,
>   Dislike of the land that you have left.
>
> My beloved rests this night
>   By the mountain ridges;
> You are fast bound by my bare hand,
>   As an iron lock upon you, O _____.
> (name of the animal)

TRANS. CM

7

THE DAGDA, also called Eochaid Ollathair, is the father of the Irish gods, the Tuatha de Danaan. He held the cauldron of hospitality from which no-one retired unsatisfied. As Ruad Rofessa, Lord of Great Knowledge, he is venerated as the supreme God of Druidry. His magical, four-sided harp, was attuned to his voice, and sang praises in his honour.

8

IN WALES, Tuesday is considered a lucky day, good for making journeys and getting married.

9

THE WELL OF SLAINE or Health was used by the Tuatha de Danaan to revive the wounded during their battle against the Fomorians. The healing god, Diancecht, and his children sang therapeutic incantations over the waters and the warriors, after submerging in the well, would emerge with their wounds whole. Many Celtic stories speak of cauldrons of healing which revive both the sick and dead: it is a feature which recurs in the medieval Grail legends where the Grail heals both the Waste Land and the Wounded King.

10

A GAELIC LEGEND about the origins of faeries tells how, at the creation, Lucifer led his rebellious angels out of heaven and that, because the gates were open, many other angels flew out also. The archangels called to the Lord, 'the heavenly city is being emptied.' So the Father ordered the gates to be shut and ordered that all that were in to stay in, and all that were out to stay out. However, those of the angelic host who had inadvertantly fallen out but who were not part of Lucifer's host had no place to go and these became the faery-folk. (C & J MATTHEWS 1993)

FEBRUARY
11

ST GOBHNAT (5TH CENTURY) was born in County Clare and fled to the Aran Islands to avoid a family feud. She was led by a vision to build a church at Kilgobnet near Dungarvan where she found nine white deer grazing. She eventually built a nunnery at Ballyvourny where she kept bees. She prevented a robber from building himself a castle by throwing a stone ball across the glen. Her well and the stone that she threw are still there and are visited by pilgrims.

FEBRUARY
12

THE STORM-DAYS OR 'WOLF-MONTH' are the first days when Spring is come but Winter still has its hold upon the land. The different forms of winds which usher in the Spring are given distinctive names:

> *Month of Faoilleach – a sharp*
> *and ravening wind.*
> *Nine days of Gearrain – a galloping wind.*
> *A week of Feadaig – a sharp*
> *and piping wind.*
> *A week of Caillich – a week of static calm*
> *Three days of Sguabaig – a soughing blast*
> *which ushers in Spring.*

FEBRUARY
13

IN THE GAULISH calendrical tablet, the Coligny Calendar, the month of January-February was called Anagantios, or 'Stay at Home time' since it was usually impossible to go far due to weather conditions.

FEBRUARY
14

DYLAN AIL TON was the child of Arianrhod. He was born precipitately when Arianrhod stepped over the magic wand of Math in order to prove her virginity. The wand being one which manifested the truth, caused the seed of her lover which was within her womb to ripen, grow and give forth all in an instant. Math adopted the child as his own, but Dylan, whose name means 'Sea, son of wave', made straight for the sea and swam away. He was accidently slain by his uncle, Gofannon, who was fashioning a spear which was fated to kill the first person to enter the forge: this was unfortunately his nephew, Dylan.

FEBRUARY
15

THIS PRAYER is a traditional soul-leading invoking the Guardian Angel to guard the soul-shrine or body and lead it forth at the point of death.

> *O Being of Brightness, Friend of Light,*
> *From the Blessed Realms of Grace,*
> *Gently encircle me, sweetly enclosing me,*
> *Guarding my soul-shrine*
> *from harm this day/night.*
>
> *Keep me from anguish,*
> *keep me from danger,*
> *Encircle my voyage over the seas.*
> *A light will you lend me, to*
> *keep and defend me,*
> *O Beautiful Being, O Guardian this night.*
>
> *Be a guiding star above me,*
> *Illuminate each rock and tide,*
> *Guide my ship across the waters,*
> *To the waveless harbourside.*

TRANS. CM

THREE DEATHS that are better than life: the death of a salmon, the death of a fat pig, the death of a robber.

CANTRE'R GWAELOD is a Welsh version of the Breton submerged city, Ys. Now situated in Cardigan Bay, it was once a series of sixteen low-lying cities which were defended by sluice-gates. One story tells how a well-maiden, Mererid, neglected her duties and caused the inundation of the land. Another tells how a drunken dyke-keeper, called Seithenyn, allowed the waters in and so drowned all save its king, Gwyddno Garanhir. Gwyddno is associated in legend with an inexhaustible hamper and with the weir in which Taliesin is discovered by Gwyddno's son, Elphin.

AWEN OR IMBAS were the respective Welsh and Irish words for inspiration. Throughout Celtic literature, we hear of the three drops of inspiration which issue from a cauldron or salmon of knowledge which brings the recipient wisdom. The awen remains a symbol of reformed druidry, showing the three drops of inspiration with a radiant pathway issuing from each drop: each pathway is said to represent the three functions of bard, ovate and druid.

THE CAIM was a protective circle, described by the hand and accompanied by an invocatory prayer; it was performed to protect people and animals, but might also be made upon oneself. The encompassing movement and prayer were used as a spiritual shield against all kinds of danger. This is Scots Gaelic caim, but any form of words can be used:

The encircling of the holy Apostles,
  The encircling of the gentle martyrs,
The encircling of the nine angels,
  About me kind, about me helping.

The encircling of quiet Brigit,
  The encircling of noble Mary,
The encircling of Michael the warrior,
  About me shielding, about me helping.

The encircling of God of the Elements,
  The encircling of Christ's loving,
The encircling of the Holy Spirit,
  About me cherish, about me helping.

TRANS. CM

45

20

ꞮRTH CUSTOMS in the west of Scotland entailed the newborn child being passed three times across the fire, then carried three times around it, always sunwise of course. Lastly the child was washed in a bowl into which a gold or silver coin had first been put. The following prayer was then spoken by the knee-woman or midwife when a child was born and acted as an informal baptism. In Celtic tradition, the ninth wave was the official demarcation beyond which exile was prescribed. The nine waves with which the child are here blessed perhaps represent the coming into incarnation of a new soul.

ᴘrayer of the Nine Waves

A little wave for your form,
  A little wave for your voice,
A little wave for your speaking.
  A little wave for your life's share,
A little wave for your giving,
  A little wave for your dowry,
A little wave for your wealth,
  A little wave for your life's time,
A little wave for your healing.
  Nine waves of grace upon you,
Waves of the Doctor of salvation.

TRANS. CM

21

N IRISH RIDDLE ASKS, 'Where is the centre of the world?' The correct answer is: 'Between your own two feet.'

22

N THE IRISH TREE ALPHABET, the letter L is represented by luis or rowan. The rowan or mountain ash has the reputation of being a powerful tree: both to repel enchantment and in many magical preparations.

23

NE OF THE THREE HARMFUL BLOWS of the Island of Britain was struck by Matholwch the Irish King upon Branwen, sister of Bran. Branwen's wedding to Matholwch was marred by the terrible insults which her brother, Efnisien, meted out to the Irish guests. Although Bran gave Matholwch the great cauldron of rebirth as the best compensation for these insults, Matholwch never forgave the Britons and caused Branwen to submit to menial tasks and to be struck daily by the butcher. Branwen trained a starling to take news of her treatment to Bran, who raised a great army and harried the Irish. Such was the devastation in the war between Ireland and Britain that followed, that Branwen died of a broken heart. She is described as one of the three great matriarchs of Britain in the triads, and is the matron of all who are constrained in unhappy marriages for the sake of their children.

WHEN AMAIRGEN GLUINGEL, the
poet of the Milesian invaders of
Ireland, first set foot on Irish soil, he
made a rhapsodic and shamanic intro-
duction of himself to the land. He
speaks of his mystical identification with
the elements, calling himself an ox who
calls out the cattle of Tethra, a bardic
kenning for the stars which seem to
arise from the sea, while the ox is a kenning for the moon.

I am a wind on the sea,
    I am a wave of the ocean,
I am the roar of the sea,
    I am an ox of seven exiles,
I am a hawk on a cliff,
    I am a tear of the sun,
I am a turning in a maze,
    I am a boar in valour,
I am a salmon in a pool,
    I am a lake on a plain,
I am a dispensing power,
    I am a power of skilful gift,
I am a grass-blade in the earth,
    subject to decay,
I am a creative, weaving god
    who counsels the head.
Who else clears the stones of a mountain?
    Who is it who declaims the sun's rising?
Who is better to tell where the sun sets?
    Who brings cattle from the house of Tethra?
Upon whom do the cattle of Tethra smile?
    Who is the ox?
Who is the weaving god who
    mends the thatch of wounds?
The incantation of a spear –
    the incantation of the wind!

TRANS. CM

CASWALLAWN, SON OF BELI, led an
insurrection while Bran was fight-
ing the Irish, and usurped the kingship.
He possessed a magical cloak of invisi-
bility which brought enchantments
upon the land until these were lifted by
Manawyddan. Caswallawn is cognate
with the historical Cassivelaunus, the
British King who fought against the
Roman invasion led by Julius Caesar.
Welsh legend tells how both men loved
one woman, Fflur (Flower), who is
clearly symbolic of the sovereignty
of Britain.

ARTHVR AND
THE STRANGE
MANTLE

26

PUNISHMENT BY ENCHANTMENT into animal shape is found in both Pagan and Christian Celtic tradition. Math ap Mathonwy causes his nephews Gwydion and Gilfaethwy to be turned into deer, pigs and wolves for a period of a year at a time; Gilfaethwy is justly turned into the female of each species for his rape of Math's virgin footholder, and Gwydion becomes the male of the species for his part in arranging the rape. Both are forced to cohabit with each other and a child is born of each union until Math disenchants them. St Columba turned the queen and son of King Aedh into cranes because they were at variance.

48

27

BADBH, WITH HER SISTERS Nemain and Macha, together make up the Morrighan, the three-fold goddess of war and death. Badbh, which means raven, often took that shape over battle-fields. She was the partner of Net, the God of Battle.

28

IN THE IRISH TREE ALPHABET, the letter F is represented by fearn or alder. In the legendary Cad Goddeu or Battle of the Trees it is described as the tree 'of pre-eminent lineage'.

29

HERE IS A HOUSE BLESSING from Scotland invoking St Bride in ver-nacular Scots: the English equivalents are given in brackets.

> Wha sains (hallows) the house the night?
>   They that sains it ilka night:
> St Bride and her brat (mantle),
>   St Colme (Columba) and his hat,
> St Michael and his spear,
>   Keep this house from the weir;
> From running thief,
>   From burning thief,
> And from a' ill Rea (evil spirit),
>   That be (by) the gate can gae;
> And from an ill wight (person)
>   That be the gate can light.

MCNEILL

The Passing of Arthur

1

Sᴛ ᴅᴀᴠɪᴅ (520–589) is the primary saint of Wales. He founded many monasteries which were run on principles of extreme simplicity and charity. St David's, Pembrokeshire, is still a place of pilgrimage where he is invoked in prayer:

'David the faithful witness of the New Law, like a bright star from heaven, shines forth in Britannia. The future greatness of Christ's servant is declared by heavenly signs: honey, water and mystic hind. O David our leader, thou strong champion, do thou also over come by thy prayers Goliath, the enemy of our earthly course.' (ᴏ'ᴍᴀʟʟᴇʏ)

2

Tʜᴇ ᴜᴛᴛᴇʀᴀɴᴄᴇ ᴀɴᴅ ᴍᴏᴠᴇᴍᴇɴᴛꜱ of crows were regarded as prophetic, as in this Scottish weather rhyme:

On the first of March
The crows begin to search;
By the first of April,
They are sitting still;
By the first of May
They're all flown away;
Crowping greedy back again,
With October's wind and rain.

ᴇᴅ. ᴍᴏɴᴛɢᴏᴍᴇʀʏ

3

Sᴛ ɴᴏɴ (6ᴛʜ ᴄᴇɴᴛᴜʀʏ) was the mother of St David. Her chapel and well, still visited to cure eye-complaints and rheumatism, is situated on the Pembrokeshire coast. Nearby is a Bronze Age stone circle; tradition tells how Non gripped one of these stones during labour and left the imprint of her fingers there.

4

Tʜʀᴇᴇ ᴀʙꜱᴇɴᴄᴇꜱ that make a house without cheer: a house without a dog, a house without a cat, a house without a baby.

5

S T CIARAN OF SAIGHIR (5TH–6TH CENTURY) was born in West Cork and educated in Europe, where he was ordained, returning to Ossory to found his monastery. He was aided by a wolf, a badger and a fox in the building work until the fox stole his shoes; the other animals fetched the fox back to be reproved and given penance by Ciaran. Saighir monastery became the burial place of the kings of Ossory.

6

E RIU (MODERN IRISH, EIRE) was the De Danaan goddess who gave her name to Ireland. When the Milesians invaded Ireland, she and sisters, Banba and Fótla were each petitioned by Amairgin, the Milesian poet, to help the Sons of Mil. He promised each goddess that her name would be the name given to the island, but it is Eriu's name that is now used.

7

T UAN, SON OF CARILL, came to Ireland with Partholon in early times. His people died of sickness, leaving him alone. As old age approached, he successively passed into the forms of a stag, a boar, a hawk and salmon until, in that shape, he was caught and eaten by a woman of Ulster from whom he was reborn as Tuan. He remembered all that had happened in Ireland and related the history of the subsequent Irish invasions by the Nemedians, the Fomorians, the Tuatha de Danaans and the Milesians to St Finnian of Moville.

8

I N WALES, Wednesday was considered to be a 'witch day' on which it was advisable to avoid any new enterprise or it would go astray. Finger and toe-nails were pared on this day.

9

M ON, THE WELSH ISLAND OF ANGLESEY, was a centre of druidic wisdom. The Romans consolidated their invasion of Britain by slaughtering the Mona druids, and outlawing druidry so that the spiritual and intellectual influence of druidry was diminished.

10

I N THE IRISH TREE ALPHABET, the letter S is represented by salle, the white willow which is the original willow to North West Europe.

MARCH
11

St Oengus the Culdee (d.c.824) was of the royal Ulster line; he lived as a hermit practising great austerities, later joining the monastery of Tallacht incognito to do menial labour. His abilities were discovered when he successfully coached an unpromising student; his abbot, Maelruain, set Oengus to help him compile the great Tallacht martyrology. The *Felire Oengusso*, Oengus' own martyrology, is a complete calendar commemorating the Irish saints and a comprehensive source-work on their lives.

MARCH
12

The protection of the gospel was sought in the Western Islands: a small saying or a verse of the Gospels was written on a piece of parchment, often illuminated, and placed in a small linen bag. It was worn by men sewn into their waistcoats, while women wore it sewn into their bodice – always under the left arm, the side of the heart. Young children wore it round their neck in a pouch, by a sacred linen cord. The wearer was considered protected against drowning, disaster, the evil eye and the assaults of Faery.

MARCH
13

The Picts were a Celtic people living in Scotland. Among the Gaels they called the Cruitne, among the Brythons the Priteni; it was the Romans who nicknamed them Picti or 'the painted people', so called because of their custom of tattooing their bodies with cruths or shapes. Cruithne was said to have settled Scotland with his seven children, after whom the regions of Scotland are still named: Cat of Caithness, Cé of Marr and Buchan, Círech of Angus and Mearns, Fiobh of Fife, Moireabh of Moray, Fótla of Atholl and Fortriu of Strathearn.

MARCH
14

In the Gaulish calendrical tablet, the Coligny Calendar, the month of February-March was called Ogronios, or 'the time of ice'.

MARCH
15

This Hebridean chant of the smooring or ritual covering of the fire invokes the Sacred Three or the Trinity:

The Sacred Three
My fortress be
Encircling me.
Come and be round
My hearth, my home.

Fend Thou my kin
And every sleeping thing within
from scathe, from sin.
Thy care our peace
Through mid of night
To light's release.

THE LADY OF THE LAKE of Arthurian tradition is identified in early texts as Morgen, the Royal Virgin of Avalon, daughter of King Afallach. She is attended by eight sister-priestesses who maintain the inviolable integrity of the mystical island of Avalon, and is the most skilled of healers. It is into her care that the wounded Arthur is bestowed after the calamitous Battle of Camlan. Her wisdom and healing care work through endless ages to restore Arthur, keeping the vessel of his life in timeless suspension, until he comes again as Rex Quondam Rexque Futurus, the Once and Future King. As she oversaw Arthur's initiation into kingship by the bestowing of the sword Excalibur, so she receives him when his kingly task is over. She is the matron of long-term illnesses and of spiritual initiations. Her attributes are a phial of ointment and the sword rising from the lake.

ST PATRICK (C.390–461) was born in Bannavem Taburniae on the west coast of Britain and was abducted to Ireland as a slave for six years. After escaping, he became a priest and returned to missionize Ireland. Despite his incomplete education, he rose to be a bishop, with his seat at Armagh. The pastoral simplicity of his teaching is epitomized by his supposed use of the shamrock to explain the mystical doctrine of the Trinity: the Three Persons in One God. His frequent depiction as a bishop casting the serpents out of Ireland may be a visual glyph of his eradication of early Celtic beliefs. Whatever the truth of the matter, there are still no snakes in Ireland. St Patrick's Day is celebrated world-wide among the Irish diaspora by 'the wearing of the green', usually a trefoil of shamrock. St Patrick is the primary patron of Ireland and of many Gaelic events. His attributes are the shamrock and the retreating snake.

BREASIL, THE HIGH KING of the other-world, lived in the farthest western ocean upon an island called Hy-Breasal. A thirteenth-century Genoese cartographer mistook it for the southwest of Ireland. Renaissance explorers of the New World believed they had found the fabled land, which is why Brazil has an Irish name to this day.

Nemetona, the Goddess of the Sacred Grove, was worshipped by the continental Celts and by the citizens of Aquae Sulis (modern Bath in Avon). Among the Romano-British, Nemetona was often partnered by Mars Rigonemetis – Mars, King of the Nemeton. A nemeton is a grove of trees which forms a sanctuary for the gods; such nemetons were the venues for ancient druidic assemblies. Nemetona is the matron of trees as well as of sacred assemblies; her attributes are a libation dish and cask of water.

St Cuthbert (634–687) was an Anglo-Saxon who was educated at the Celtic monastery of Melrose, one of many Anglo-Saxon saints who had a Celtic education and who sought to reconcile both peoples in the peace of Christ. He was consecrated bishop of Lindisfarne rather against his natural inclination to live a hermetic existence on the Inner Farne Island. His dying words are a testament of peace: 'Always preserve divine charity among yourselves, and when you come together to discuss your common affairs let your principal goal be to reach a unanimous decision.'

The spring equinox is called Alban Eiler or 'The Light of the Earth' among the reformed orders of druidry. It marks the mid-point between the sun's least and strongest appearance at Midwinter and Midsummer, respectively. Now the sun is welcomed with glad heart, for its lancing rays awaken the seemingly dead earth to new life and signals the ending of the long, cold winter. In this Scots Gaelic chant to welcome the sun, the female gender is retained, for the feminine sun is common to the earliest beliefs of North-West Europe.

Welcome to you, sun of the seasons' turning,
In your circuit of the high heavens;
Strong are your steps on the unfurled heights,
Glad Mother are you to the constellations.

You sink down into the ocean of want,
Without defeat and without scathe;
You rise up on the peaceful wave
Like a queen in her maidenhood's flower.

TRANS. CM

MARCH
22

THE GAELS accorded special qualities to each of the five provinces of Ireland. The East was considered to be a place of plenty, of supplies, bee-hives, contests, feats of arms, householders, nobles, abundance, dignity, strength, wealth, householding, arts, accoutrements, treasures, satin, serge, cloth and hospitality. The province of Leinster, which includes modern Dublin, still retains the reputation for being a cosmopolitan and well-established centre for trade and cultural exchange. (*See 20 & 26 June, 20 September and 20 December for the other provinces.*)

MARCH
23

THE NATIVE NORTHERN BRITISH GOD, Cocidius, was equated by the Romans with Mars. He is depicted as a hunter or as a warrior with spear and shield. One dedication calls him Cocidius Vernostonus or Cocidius of the Aldar Tree: this may be a reinforcement of the underlying meaning of his name of 'the Red One', since aldar bark is a dark red colour, an allusion to his warlike and hunting abilities.

MARCH
24

EVERY CELTIC TRIBE seems to have set up a pillar-stone or venerated a sacred tree in the middle of its tribal lands. This pillar or tree acted as a landmark and a locus of power, as a rallying point for tribal assembly, to be treated with honour and kept from the depredations of enemies. Many tree customs still practised today are remnants of such veneration.

MARCH
25

LADY-DAY IS DEDICATED to Lady Mary the Virgin. Here she is invoked by the 9th-century cleric, Blathmac:

> *Mary, sun of our race, come to us,*
> *That we may welcome the compassion*
> *of a whole heart.*
> *Well for us that you bore*
> *the summer-lord, Jesus:*
> *He slept in your womb a while,*
> *Though he existed before your*
> *own conception.*
> *Sun of women, it is true what we have said,*
> *You are virgin after childbirth,*
> *queen and holy maiden.*

BLATHMAC

MABON AP MODRON is the British God of Youth. His name is strictly a title which means 'Son, son of Mother' and his cult is shrouded in antiquitity. He was stolen 'from between his mother and wall' when he was only three nights old and is lost in time. One of Culhwch's impossible tasks to recover Mabon, which he does by the help of the oldest animals. Through the chain of memory constructed from the individual memories of a blackbird, stag, owl, eagle and salmon, Mabon is recovered from his imprisonment at Caer Loyw or Gloucester.

GEASA OR PROHIBITIONS were entwined with the destiny and lifestyle of many prominant Celtic figures; these could not be broken without threatening their life. Some kings and heroes were often crippled by such geasa, as was King Conaire whose nine geasa included not being able to go deosil round his own palace of Tara nor leave it for more than nine nights. The bonds of the geasa, though restrictive in many ways, seem to have maintained important boundaries between worldly and otherworldly realms.

ANEIRIN IS COUNTED as one of the Cynfeirdd, the earliest British poets. His greatest poem, Y Gododdin tells how, at the battle of Catraeth (600 AD), a British warband led by Mynyddawg Mwynfawr, was vanquished by the English. Each stanza eulogizes a war-leader who fell: this one speaks of Buddfan ap Bleiddfan.

Hero of the covering shield,
* his grey brows under,*
Fluid as a charger,
* On the battle-slope he was a tumult, a fire;*
Spear-swift he was and radiant:
* Raven-fodder he became, the prey of crows.*
Before his raptor threw him at the ford
* At dew-fall, an eagle of masterly*
* movement was he,*
Near the seaspray by the hill:
* The world's poets judged him*
* as the heart of mankind.*

TRANS. CM

HOSPITALITY WAS CONSIDERED to be a primary celtic virtue. Whoever ate at your table was as a kinsman, his life inviolate. To receive a guest as a sacred trust is the advice of the monastic *Book of Cerne*:

I saw a stranger yestreen,
I put food in the eating place,
drink in the drinking place,
music in the listening place,
and in the sacred name of the Triune,
He blessed myself and my house,
my cattle and my dear ones,
and the lark said in her song
often, often, often goes Christ
in the stranger's guise.

ED. O'MALLEY

IN THE IRISH TREE ALPHABET, the letter N is represented by nuin or ash.

THIS ANONYMOUS IRISH POEM speaks of the Crucifixion:

At the cry of the first bird
  They began to crucify Thee,
O cheek like a swan.
  It were not right ever to cease lamenting –
It was like the parting of day from night.

Ah! though sore the suffering
  Put upon the body of Mary's Son –
Sorer to Him was the grief
  That was upon her for His sake.

TRANS. MEYER

57

The Combat of the Red and White Dragons

THIS POEM FROM *The Book of Leinster* celebrates the birds of the year and their associated saints-days: Abbot Maelruan of Tallaght (7th July), St Ruadan (15th April), St Ciaran of Clonmacnoise (9th Sept) the son of a chariot-maker, and St Cyprian (16th Sept):

Birds of the world,
    bright without shame
it is to welcome the sun again;
    at the nones of January,
whatever the hour,
    a host consorts in the
sheltering wood.

On the eighth of the calends
    of eminent April
Flights of swallows
    make congregation;
a strand of exile their concealment
    from the eighth of the
calends of October.

On the feast of Ruadan,
    runs the saying,
all their fetters are unlocked
    from Winter's hell.
On the seventeenth of the
    calends of May,
unceasing cuckoos
    throng the wood.

In Tallaght the birds relent their
    Sung music on the July calends
for Mael Ruan, whom the Badbh took not:
        the living pray on that
        woeful day.

On Ciaran's feast,
    son of the smith,
the barnacle goose flies
    over cold oceans;
on Cyprian's feast,
    a great contention,
the brown stag bells
    from the red plains.

Three score thousand years
    of whiteness
is the term of the world,
    without doubt;
billows will burst across every airt
    at the end of night,
at the cry of birds.

Renewing is the melodious music
    of birds to the King of
the bright clouds,
    their praise to the
King of stars:
    listen to the feathered
choir afar!

TRANS. CM

59

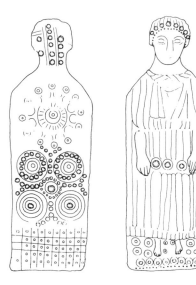

THE SUN IS UNIVERSALLY CELEBRATED in Celtic lore, though specifically solar deities are rare. The symbols of wheel and triskel echo the rolling motion of the sun through the sky and it is significant that egg or cheese-rolling customs still abound at Easter-time. Solar diadems and helmets have been excavated, pointing to a solar cult. The Irish deities Lugh, Aine and Brighid all have solar aspects to their cult, as do the British deities Beli, Lleu and Sul.

IN THE GAULISH CALENDRICAL TABLET, the Coligny Calendar, the month of March-April was called Cutios, 'the time of winds'.

IN NORTHERN IRELAND, the first nine days of April were called 'the Borrowed Days' because March is said to borrow nine days from April: 'three to fleece the blackbird, three to punish the stone-chat, three days for the grey cow.' (DANAHER)

THREE THINGS THAT COME UNBIDDEN: fear, jealousy and love.

MADE OF THE ENCHANTED CRANE-SKIN of the faery woman, Aoife, the Crane Bag was a receptacle for many wonder-working treasures: the shirt and knife of Manannan, the girdle and hook of Goibniu the smith, the King of Scotland's shears, the King of Lochlainn's helmet, the bones of Asal's pigs. These seven objects could only be discovered at high tide; at low tide, the Crane Bag would appear empty. Equipped with these objects, the owner possessed miraculous powers which would see him through the world. Made by Manannan, it came briefly into mortal hands, including those of Fionn Mac Cumhail, before returning to Manannan again. The Crane Bag is one of many sacred objects or hallows which are the object of quest and adventure.

APRIL
7

THE VIATICUM OF LLEFOED WYNEBGLAWR is a Welsh poet's book of lore, describing many matters:

In spring the land is partly bare,
If people are turbulent,
*   their shout is deceitful.*
In calm reflection riches are despised.
What is not often seen is neglected.

ED. SKENE

APRIL
8

IN WALES, Thursday was not a day to move house, since it was said the birds never carried anything to their nests on this day, although it was a good day for a christening.

APRIL
9

ST MADRUN (5TH CENTURY) also called Materiana, was the daughter of Vortigern and wife of Ynyr Gwent of Caerwent. She fled with her son Ceidio to Carn Fadryn and then to Boscastle, Cornwall where she was buried. Aspects of her legend are strikingly resonant with that of Modron, mother of Mabon.

APRIL
10

THE IRISH CLERIC, Sedulius Scottus, was born Siadhal mac Feredach, in about 820 AD. He was also a fine poet as this poem on Easter Sunday written to Tado, Archbishop of Milan, proclaims:

Christ the true Sun rose
*   from the dark last night,*
The mystic harvest of the Lord's own field.
*   Now wandering tribes of bees joyously sport*
Between the flowers,
*   seeking their nectars sweet.*
The honeyed winds with
*   birdsong are bedewed,*
Nocturnal melody of nightingales abounds.
*   In church, the people chorus*
out their Sion song,
*   Their hundred-folded alleluia sounds.*
Tado, our father, may heavenly Easter joy
*   Gather you to the threshold of the light.*

TRANS. CM

Nehelenia was a celtic goddess venerated on both sides of the North Sea, in Britain and Holland. She is the matron of sea-farers and travellers and her name means 'the Steerswoman'. She is depicted accompanied by a dog, and with marine imagery such as a prow, oar or ship's rope.

The transmigration of the soul is clearly seen in Celtic lore: the life of the body is not the end of the soul, which is understood to take other forms successively. *Cormac's Glossary* speaks of the tuirgen or circuit of births which the soul passes through: 'the birth that passes from every nature into another; a transitory birth which has traversed all nature from Adam and goes through every wonderful time down to the world's doom, giving the nature of one life.' (CM 1989)

Children in Ireland in the 19th century used to set bowls of water on the floor of their homes, there to catch the sun's rays at Easter-time, a festival which can only fall between 26th March–22nd April. In Scotland and South Wales, people were advised to rise early and go to the hilltops before sunrise to see the sun-dancing or para-helion, a natural phenomena by which the sun seems to dance.

Three smiles that are worse than grief: the smile of melting snow, the smile of your partner after sleeping with another, the smile of a leaping dog.

ST PADARN (5TH–6TH CENTURY) was the founder of Llanbadarn Fawr in Dyfed. His other monastic foundations are all situated along Roman roads. Arthur craved Padarn's tunic but the saint subdued him by commanding the earth to swallow the erring king up to his chin. Padarn's crozier, Cyrwen, had the power to subdue embattled armies.

THE CURIOUS CUSTOM OF BUNDLING was quite common in Wales among courting couples who were permitted to remove their shoes and spend the evening reclining on the bed in conversation, usually strictly separated by individual bed-coverings. Although bundling was supposed to be a preparation for marriage, it did not always follow, but, under the humane laws of Hywel Dda (D.950), the rights of women and of bastard children's inheritance were maintained, so that, even if the couple went further than conversation, it was not considered to be a terminal loss of honour. Bundling was also common in other parts of Europe and was a sensible method of courting during the winter months

This advice when going among strangers comes from *The Instructions of Cormac*, the King of Ireland who is called 'the Irish Solomon':

Be not too wise, not too foolish,
*   be not too conceited, nor too diffident,*
be not too haughty, nor too humble,
*   be not too talkative, nor too silent,*
be not too hard, nor too feeble.

If you be too wise, one will expect
*   too much of you;*
if you be too foolish, you will be deceived;
*   if you be too conceited,*
you will be thought vexatious;
*   if you be too talkative,*
you will not be heeded;
*   if you be too silent, you will not be regarded;*
if you be too hard, you will be broken;
*   if you be too feeble, you will be crushed.*

TRANS. MEYER

APRIL
18

THREE IMPOSSIBLE MIXTURES until the world's doom: that ogham and pillar be blent together, that heaven and earth be blent together, that sun and moon be blent together.

APRIL
19

DRUIDIC JUDGEMENTS were often concluded with the help of certain ordeals. Legend speaks of the twelve ordeals of Morann mac Maine. One of these ordeals was that of the caul in which he had been born: if it were put about the neck of a guilty person it would choke him; whereas it would expand round the neck of the innocent.

APRIL
20

THE AFANC WAS A LEGENDARY MONSTER that lived in Llyn Llion and lurked in the Welsh imagination as Nessie does in Loch Ness and the Scottish mind. It was believed to be a giant beaver which was responsible for the overflow of the lake. The legendary hero, Hu Gadarn, harnessed two horned oxen to pull it out of the lake. These oxen appear to be cosmological beasts, and appear in many Welsh poems as the planetary companions and helpers of heroes who overcome magical enchantments which plague the land.

APRIL
21

ST BEUNO (6TH CENTURY) lived in North Wales. He is said to have raised seven people from the dead, including his niece Gwenfrewi. He planted an acorn on his father's grave which grew to be a mighty oak. According to local lore, any Englishman who passed between the trunk of this tree and its branch died, whereas Welshmen passed through safely. When Beuno lay dying, his last words were, 'I see the Holy Trinity and the saints and druids.' (ELLIS)

APRIL
22

THE ISLAND OF GWALES (Grassholm, Pembrokeshire) is where the head of Bran the Blessed was brought by his seven remaining followers. The Birds of Rhiannon sang to bring forgetfulness of their grief, while the head of Bran itself regaled them for eighty years, talking as naturally in death as it had in life.

23

IN THE WESTERN HIGHLANDS of Scotland, young girls wore a snood or white band of ribbon around their heads in token of maidenhood. This was replaced on marriage by the kertch, a square of fine linen which was pleated into three points to become 'the shapely coif of three crowns', in token of the Trinity. The women gathered about the newly kertched wife and sang:

> Your wedding crown you have put on,
>   Often it has brought glory to woman;
> Be virtuous but also gracious,
>   Be clear in word and deed.
>
> Be hospitable but also wise,
>   Be courageous but also calm,
> Be frank but also reserved,
>   Be just but also generous.

ED. CARMICHAEL

24

THE CUMULATIVE LIFE-SPANS of the Oldest Animals brought the Celts remembrance of ancestral and legendary eras. Time-cycles are remembered in this Irish saying:

> Three life-times of the
>   Stag for the Blackbird;
> three life-times of the Blackbird for the Eagle;
>   three life-times of the Eagle for the Salmon;
> three life-times of the Salmon for the Yew.

CM 1987

25

THE VIATICUM of Llefoed Wyneb-glawr continues:

> Watch-stones form the best history.
>   The wisdom of a host, and   .
>   deception through laughter.
> Let fundamental knowledge be accurate …
>   Except God, there is no one
>   that knows the future.

26

IN THE GAULISH CALENDRICAL TABLET, the Coligny Calendar, the month of April-May was called Giamonios or 'shoots-show', as Spring passes into early Summer.

27

Ⓣ HIS PREPARATION for the soul's journey is from the *Black Book of
Caermathan*:

> *Let us not reproach one another,*
> *but rather mutually save ourselves.*
> *Certain is a meeting after separation,*
> *The appointment of a senate,*
> *and a certain conference,*
> *And the rising from the grave*
> *after a long repose ...*
> *To the place where there are flowers*
> *and dew on the pleasant land,*
> *Where there are singers tuning*
> *their harmonious lays.*

ED. SKENE

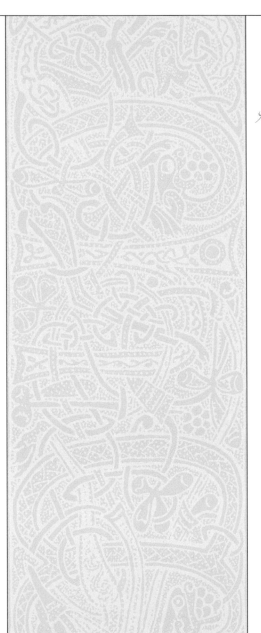

28

Ⓛ LUDD, SON OF BELI, is the founder of
London where his name is still
remembered at Ludgate. With the help
of his brother, Llefelys, he overcame
three oppressions: an intrusive otherworldly race called the Coraneid, two
battling dragons and the loss of his
household's food-store by a giant. These
tasks are fulfilled at the critical time of
Beltane when the winter half of the
year succeeds to the summer half.

ONE OF LLUDD'S TASKS is to discover what makes a terrible scream each May-Eve, rendering infertile his kingdom. He discovers that the cause is two warring dragons. By finding the middle of the land, at Rhydychen (Oxford), and luring them into a chest when they fall to rest, he captures them and is able to bury them in Snowdonia. These same dragons are those which are later released by Merlin when Vortigern attempts to build a tower over their burial place. They signify the energy of the land and are abroad at Beltane; only a worthy monarch can utilize their power in a safe way. Their release coincides with the coming of the Pendragon clan.

THIS IS THE DAY on which the great poet Taliesin is washed into Gwyddno's weir and found by Elphin. As the boy, Gwion, he tends Ceridwen's cauldron of knowledge until he accidently splashes its liquor on his finger and receives all knowledge. He flees as a hare, a fish, a bird and a grain of wheat, to be pursued by Ceridwen as a greyhound, an otter and a hawk. As a hen, she eats Taliesin as a grain of wheat and he is reborn of her womb. He is the primary chief poet of the Island of Britain and enters the service of Elphin and then Arthur, with whom he enters Annwn in the ship Prydwen. The glorious festival of Beltane has come: everyone remains wakeful to welcome in the May and to greet the dawn with songs of joy.

BELTANE

SUMMER'S SONG

Beltane celebrates the coming of summer's warmth and the return to outdoor gatherings and celebrations. During this season, the growing cycle enters its mature, burgeoning stage when the trees are in full leaf and the many-coloured flowers are fully illuminated by strong sunlight. There are pleasure, plenty and pastimes to be enjoyed. It is a time of love and adventure, inspired by the fledging birds which leave the nest at this time to find their own territory. Beltane encourages us to fully engage in the projects and plans which we have waited a long winter to fulfil.

The Grail Quest

BELTANE CELEBRATES the bright half of the year and was warmly welcomed for it was the official beginning of summer when over-wintered animals could be driven out into wider pasturing, and when scattered households would meet together and travel forth. It also marked the official start of the campaigning season. The festival, whose name means 'the fires of Bel' is named after Beli or Belenus, the shining one, an archaic god for whom no legend remains. Several inscriptions remain to the Romano-Celtic Apollo Belenus, testifying to the solar and healing qualities of the original Celtic god.

On Beltane Eve, fire was kindled afresh, in some parts by means of nine men taking nine different woods and making fire by the friction of a fire drill. Two separate bonfires were made from this flame and all domestic animals and peoples were driven between them, to purge all life of winter diseases and any misfortunes associated with the dark or Samhain half of the year. That this was an ordeal is remembered in the Scots Gaelic expression 'hotter than the fires of Beul'. Brands kindled at the

Beltane fires were borne to each household to rekindle all household lights and fires, which had been previously extinguished in preparation for the coming of the new light. The kindling of the Beltane fire was anciently the preserve of the druids: no one else would presume to raise their fire before the local Beltane fire had been kindled. St Patrick, however, kindled the Paschal Fire prior to the celebration of Beltane: an act which the indigenous druids considered presumptuous.

The festival of Beltane represented all things that were held in low esteem by the Church and which were notably absent from traditional ecclesiastical celebration: sexuality, eros, dancing and singing. It was anciently customary for unmarried couples and sweethearts to pair off and go to the woods on Beltane eve, so that the month of May has become proverbial for sexual initiation and loving activity. The festival of Imbolc, occurring nine months later, is perhaps not insignificantly associated with child-birth, and midwifery!

Of all the Celtic festivals, Beltane is still the most enthusiastically celebrated throughout Britain and Ireland. There are few villages that do not have their own local May-Day rituals and customs. Dancing, processions, singing, the election of a May Queen and King, and other customs are commonly celebrated.

71

MAY
2

ALL CELTIC PEOPLES are united in their adherence to walking, stirring or blessing in the *deosil* or sunwise direction. Fishermen in Wales turned their boats *deosil* to bless their day's work. *Deosil* derives from 'moving to the right'. At pilgrimage points all over the Celtic world, it is customary to 'make a sunwise circuit' of the site while reciting the prescribed prayers associated with the saint of that place.

MAY
3

THROUGHOUT ROMANO-CELTIC EUROPE, the Triple Mothers were worshipped as the Deae Matres or Matronae. They are usually depicted as seated, mature figures carrying fruits, bread and babies and were clearly venerated by all sections of society. Triple deities abound in Celtic tradition, as we find in the triple Morrigan, the triple Brighid and the threefold Goddesses of Irish Sovereignty – Fótla, Eriu and Banba. The Celtic preoccupation with threefold groupings is seen from the tripling of divine powers to threefold repetitions of invocations and prayers. The number three is still predominant in British and Irish culture as being lucky, and significant events are believed 'to come in threes'.

MAY
4

THE CADI HAF is a traditional character from Welsh May Day customs when the Summer Branch is borne about the locality by dancers. The Cadi Haf is attired in a man's coat and woman's petticoat, with a blackened face, representing the He-She. The Man-Woman or He-She is an important figure in folklore, representing the non-duality of the otherworld, allowing humour and paradox to crack apart the formal texture of everyday life. The companies of dancers that go about at May-time are the celebrants of the summer, just as the Guisers are the celebrants of winter.

MAY
5

THREE SLENDER THINGS that best support the world: the slender stream of milk from the cow's dug into the pail; the slender blade of green corn upon the ground; the slender thread over the hand of a skilled woman. (MEYER)

MAY
6

THIS BLESSING FOR A LOVER comes from Gaelic Scotland:

You are the star of each night,
  You are the brightness of every morning,
You are the story of each guest,
  You are the report of every land.

No evil shall befall you,
  On hill nor bank,
In field or valley,
  On mountain or in glen.

Neither above nor below,
  Neither in sea nor on shore,
In skies above,
  Nor in the depths.

You are the kernel of my heart,
  You are the face of my sun,
You are the harp of my music,
  You are the crown of my company.

TRANS. CM

MAY
7

THE VIATICUM of Llefoed Wyneb-glawr continues:

Trees have put on a beauteous robe.
A mirror is not visible in the dark.
A candle will not preserve from cold.
He is not happy who is not discreet.

MAY
8

IN WALES, Friday was the most unlucky day, the very one on which Adam and Eve were expelled from Eden. Fruit-trees pruned on Friday would not blossom for three years. The waters of lakes, streams and rivers were controlled by faeries on Fridays.

MAY
9

YNYS ENLLI or Bardsey Island, off the Lleyn peninsula in Wales, is called the Island of Saints. It is the traditional place of Myrddin's (Merlin's) retirement, from whence he guards the treasures or hallowed objects of Britain. The island of Britain itself is called 'Myrddin's Enclosure' in Welsh lore.

MAY
10

GWALCHMAI AP GWYAR was the nephew of Arthur, better known from medieval legend as Gawain. His name means 'the Hawk of May'. He was the epitomy of virtue and courtesy and is listed in the Triads as one of the three best men with guests and visitors from afar; he achieves more by his courtesy than others achieve by deeds of arms. Gwalchmai/Gawain is unequalled as the champion of women and the Goddess. (J MATTHEWS 1990)

MAY
11

THE ANCIENT CELTS bound themselves by the greatest oath of allegiance, calling upon the elements to witness it, 'May we keep faith or let the sky fall and crush, the earth open and swallow us, or the sea rise up and overwhelm us.' At the coming of Christianity, a common title for God and Jesus was significantly 'King of the Elements': only by acknowledging a power stronger than that of the elements could the Celts reconcile their ancient dread of elemental catastrophe.

73

MAY
12

IN THE IRISH TREE ALPHABET, the letter H is represented by hawthorn. The hawthorn is associated with the sexual licence of the Beltane quarter due to the overpowering pheromonal scent of its blossoms at this time. It is the one tree which is overwhelmingly associated with the outdoors, with faeries and with sexual sportiveness: its shoots are never brought indoors for fear of overwhelming the orderliness of everyday life.

BRAN THE BLESSED, son of Llyr was the titanic king of Britain who gave his sister Branwen in marriage to the King of Ireland. To atone for the insulting behaviour of his brother to the Irish, Bran also gave them the cauldron of rebirth into which dead soldiers could be put and brought forth alive but unspeaking.

In the war which ensued when he came to rescue his sister from Irish mal-treatment, the Irish used this cauldron to devastating effect against the British. In the combat, Bran was wounded and ordered that his followers behead him and bury the head at the White Mount in London. On their way thither, his men stopped at two otherworldly locations where they remained for many years; during this time, the head of Bran conversed with his men and the birds of Rhiannon sang forgetfulness of the fray. His head was buried facing France to fend off invasion, at the point now occupied by the Tower of London which still remembers Bran, whose name means 'raven', in the legend of its protecting ravens whose presence is said to similarly fend off the invasion of Britain.

74

THE TRAINING OF THE WARRIOR was a long task, frequently undertaken by warrior-women who were responsible for teaching boys the arts of combat and love. This empowerment may be compared with the nine wishes gifted upon the newborn child on 20 Feb, since it is yet another ninefold chant: it calls upon the hero Cuchulainn and upon the legendary hosts of Fionn Mac Cumhail, the Fianna:

Power of eye upon you,
  Power of the elements upon you,
Power of my heart's wish.

Power of ebb upon you,
  Power of flow upon you,
Power of my seasoned fellowship.

Power of King Cù Chulainn upon you,
  Power of the king of the world upon you,
Power of the king of the Fianna.

ED. CARMICHAEL

IN THE GAULISH CALENDRICAL TABLET, the Coligny Calendar, the month of May-June was called Simivisionios, or 'the time of brightness', as the rays of the sun begin to drench the land with their perpendicular spears of light.

ST BRENDAN (C.486–575) abbot of Clonfert is most particularly remembered for his famous immram or otherworldly voyage in search of the Land of Saints across the Atlantic Ocean, during which he celebrated mass on a whale's back. His reputation as a great traveller is not misplaced, since he visited St Columba on Iona and is said to have gone to Brittany with St Malo. He is known as 'Brendan the Navigator'.

OGHAM WAS A MEANS OF INSCRIPTION formed by notching the edge of a stone-pillar or twig. Many pillar-stones with ogham inscriptions survive in Ireland and West Wales, usually as grave or boundary markers. The druids and poets used ogham in magical, divinatory and encoded ways. Each ogham mark was called by the name of a tree, causing it to be also called 'the tree alphabet'. The names for the modern Irish alphabet still use these tree names. Attempts have been made to equate the ogham row with a calendrical method of reckoning, but this was not customary in ancient tradition.

THE TYLWYTH TEG or 'the fair folk' is the name given to the faeries in Wales. In common with the faery folk elsewhere they are averse to iron, are willing to co-operate with humankind in exchange for a few simple gifts and boldly proposition midwives to go with them to aid faery mothers.

THE SUPREME Welsh love-poet, Dafydd ap Gwylym (FL.1320–70) described himself as 'Ovid's man'. He writes here about the pursuit of his current sweetheart and the retreat which nature offers to them:

It was sweet, sweetheart, a while
  Beneath the birchgrove's shade to live.
To cuddle up was even sweeter,
  In the wood's retreat close hidden,
Wandering hand in hand along the sea-shore,
  Lingering hand in hand along the
wood-shore...
Lying beside each other in the grove,
  Mutually shunning folk, complicit in
complaint,
Living together with kindness, quaffing mead,
  Resting in each other's love, one heart,
Keeping tryst with love's secret.

TRANS. CM

THE MAY-DAY CELEBRATIONS at Padstow in Cornwall retain the fullest vigour of Beltane customs. After serenading the town through midnight and the small hours, the Mayers re-emerge with the Oss – a fearsome pointy-beaked hobby horse which covers its wearer by a six-foot hoop covered with black tarpaulin. It processes the streets, led on by its Teaser, a white-clad Mayer. Its dance dives and swoops, ever seeking for a young woman to bring under its skirts: to be the object of the Oss is considered to grant fertility and to be lucky. The chorus of the Padstow May-Day song goes:

Unite and unite and let us unite,
  For Summer is acome unto day
And whither we are going we will all unite
  On the merry morning of May.

KIGHTLY

ST COLLEN was the founder of Llangollen in Clwyd. His many legends speak of him as a fierce suppressor of ancient beliefs, notably he is reported to have had a combat with Gwyn ap Nudd, the otherworldly king, at his palace under Glastonbury Tor.

MAY 22

ON CLEAR NIGHTS, we can some-times see the Milky Way. In Wales the Milky Way is known as Caer Gwydion; in Gaelic it is called Bothar na Bo Finne (Road of the White Cow). It is significant that the myths of the Milky Way in Celtic countries seem to adhere to the reiving of animals: Gwydion steals the swine of Annwn, and both Irish and British legend speak of the theft of the otherworldly Cow/Bull. The cow was the object of ancient quest, giving milk, goodness, life, restoration, immortality, soma etc. The Milky Way is known throughout Europe as a galactic pilgrimage route, being called, in Britain, the Walsingham Way and in Spain, El Camino de Santiago, the road to Compostella.

MAY 23

BELTANE was the traditional time for warfare, feuding and raiding to commence. The roving troops of the fianna led by Fionn Mac Cumhail lived off the land from Beltane to Samhain, while from Samhain to Beltane they were billeted upon and maintained by the people.

MAY 24

BARINTHUS IS THE FERRYMAN who, in the company of Merlin and Talie-sin, bears Arthur over to Avalon. He is associated with St Barrind of Northern Ireland, who is the mentor of St Brendan and the inspirer of his voyage.

MAY 25

THIS WELSH POEM-PRAYER is uttered by a recently-bereaved cleric:

May-time, fairest season;
* noisy are the birds,*
green the woods,
* the ploughs are in the furrow,*
the ox in the yoke,
* green is the sea,*
the lands grow many-coloured.

When the cuckoos sing on the
* tops of the splendid trees,*
my wretchedness grows greater;
* my breath is painful,*
my distress is manifest,
* since my kinsmen have passed away....*

The gift I ask,
* may it not be denied me,*
peace between me and God;
* may I find the road to the Gate of Glory,*
Christ, may I not be sad before Thy throne.

CM 1994

MAY 26

WHEN MIDIR SOUGHT TO WOO his reincarnated wife, Etain, back to the otherworld, he sang her this song:

Fair lady, will you go with me to the
wonderous land of stars?
In that land, hair is yellow as primroses,
skin the colour of snow.
There, neither 'mine' nor 'yours' is
heard. Teeth are white, brows are black.
Our hosts are a delight to the eye, every
cheek is of foxglove's hue.
Sweet streams water the earth there. We
drink the best mead and wine. Each of us
is of gentle lineage; conception is without
guilt or sin amongst us.

TRANS. CM

MAY 27

THE CELTIC CHURCH recognized three forms of martyrdom: the red mar-tyrdom of death for Christ's sake, the green martyrdom of renunciation of one's former lifestyle and the white martyrdom of exile from home and family, as expressed by King Cormac mac Cuileannáin of Munster:

Shall I go, O King of the Mysteries,
* After my fill of music and cushions,*
To turn my face to the shore,
* My back on my native land?*

TRANS. MEYER

URING MAY, Creiddylad, the betrothed of Gwythyr ap Greidawl, was carried off by the God of the Underworld, Gwyn ap Nudd. The case was brought to Arthur who judged that Creiddylad should return to her house and that Gwyn and Gwythyr should combat for her every May-Day until doomsday. Until the early nineteenth century, the people of South Wales enacted the ritual abduction of Creiddylad with two sets of contestants in memory of this event and in celebration of May.

RBOR DAY is celebrated in Aston-on-Clun in Shropshire where the rare, black poplar tree is freshly decorated and honoured. Although the date of this festival coincides with Oak-Apple Day – established on 29th May 1660, the 30th birthday of King Charles II, to celebrate the restoration of the monarchy, and incidentally of the May customs that had been banned under the Commonwealth – the decorating and honouring of trees is an ancient Celtic custom.

OIBHNIU WAS THE IRISH GOD of Smithcraft. A similar myth surrounds his British counterpart, Gofannon: that he created a deadly spear which had to be cast at the first person to enter the forge, which happened to be his nephew. Goibhniu slew Ruadan, son of Brighid, while Gofannon slew Dylan. Goibhniu presides over a feast whose ale exempts all feasters from death and disease.

ERE THE IRISH BEAUTY, Grainne sings, perhaps somewhat reproachfully, to her sleeping beloved, Diarmuid, with whom she eloped:

The stag in the east sleeps not;
he ceases not his bellow;
even though he steps in the blackbirds' grove,
sleep is the last thing on his mind.

The hornless hind sleeps not,
but cries for her speckled fawn;
she speeds over the scrub
and sleeps not in her holt.

The melodious linnet sleeps not in
the tangled tree tops; great song make
they in the wood, even the thrush sleeps not.

The well-fed duck sleeps not,
but swims her circuit; she neither stays
nor stops, and in her nest she sleeps not.

Tonight the curlew sleeps not
over the wild tempest raging;
sweet is the sound of his clear voice,
he sleeps not in the stream.

TRANS. CM

The Campaigns of the Fianna

THE IRISH HERO, Bran mac Febal, was approached by a faery woman who shook her silver branch at him so that he fell into a deep trance; while he slept, she sang an invitation for him to visit the otherworld:

Do not fall on a bed of sloth,
  Let not intoxication overcome you,
Begin a voyage across the clear sea,
  If perchance you may reach the
Land of Women.

He sailed to the realm of Manannan and enjoyed his stay in the Land of Women, but when he and his men attempted to return to Ireland, the first man to reach the shore fell to dust, so long had they been absent.

FINNECES WAS the poetic teacher of Fionn Mac Cumhail. It had been prophesied that Finneces (White Wisdom) would catch the salmon of knowledge, but he set the young Fionn to cook it. As the fire grew hotter, so the fish-juice spat out onto Fionn's thumb which he swiftly thrust into his mouth to cool, thus receiving all knowledge. This story is an Irish parallel to that of Taliesin's.

ST KEVIN OR COEMGEN (D.618) founded the abbey of Glendalough in Co. Wicklow where he had his first hermitage. So still was he in prayer that a blackbird nested on his hand and laid her egg. He is said to have fed his community with salmon which an otter fished for him.

THE CUSTOM of well-dressing goes back to Celtic antiquity, but is still maintained in the villages of Derbyshire, whose limestone peaks harbour many springs. Dressed during the summer months, the many wells each receive a clay-soaked frame upon which images are made with dyes, lichens, barks, mosses and flowers. The custom has survived due to the Church's endorsement; a service of blessing the wells is usually conducted on erection of the frame and a majority of present-day images depict religious themes.

JUNE
5

THREE GLORIES of a gathering: a beautiful wife, a good horse, a swift hound. (MEYER)

JUNE
6

DIANCECHT WAS THE DOCTOR of the Irish invaders, the Tuatha de Danaan. He created a mechanical silver hand for King Nuadu, after he lost it in battle, but Diancecht's son, Miach, was able to create a new hand of flesh. In jealousy, Diancecht struck his son three times, but still he recovered; lastly, he cut out his brain and Miach died. Miach's sister, Airmed, saw how three hundred and sixty-five herbs grew out of his joints and sinews and gathered these together in her mantle, but Diancecht confused the herbs, so that their properties were unclear.

JUNE
7

THE VIATICUM of Llefoed Wyneb-glawr continues:

*Empty the country where
 there is no religion.
The unbeliever does not think of God.
 No one that does not improve
is called skilful.
 Let us observe and acquire religion.*

JUNE
8

IN WALES, Saturday was a fortunate day, especially as a market-day for poultry, butter, cheese and meat. The property of a bride and groom were always conveyed to their new house on a Saturday, although marriages were never contracted on this day lest the pair not live to see out the year.

9

S T COLUMBA (521-97) was born in Donegal of the royal Ui Neill line. His turbulent and argumentative nature brought about his exile from Ireland, and he made his foundation on Iona. He converted Brude, King of the Picts and his monks missionized and taught all over Scotland. He returned to Ireland for the Convention of Druim-Cetta at the petition of the poets, whose privileges threatened to be considerably curtailed thereat. This was but one instance of Columba's innate respect for ancient Celtic custom; he likewise maintained the sanctity of the oak-groves of Derry. This Dies Irae comes from Columba's long poem, *Altus Prosator*, and speaks of doomsday:

> The reign of the righteous king,
>   The day of the lord is nigh,
> Day of wrath and vengeance,
>   Of shadow and insubstantiality.
> The wondrous end-day comes,
>   Strong with thundering,
> The augured day of anguish,
>   Bitterness and lamentation,
> On which will cease woman's
>   Fair love and sweet desire;
> Contention, man with man, shall cease,
>   And worldly lusts no more increase.

TRANS. CM

81

IN THE IRISH TREE ALPHABET, the letter D is represented by duir or oak. The word, druid, comes from the same root as oak and may mean 'oak-sage'.

THIS TRADITIONAL IRISH BLESSING of a bride and groom lovingly maintains the spirit of Beltane in the marriage:

> *Length of life and sunny days,*
> *and may your souls not go homewards*
> *til your own child falls in love!*

THE BAKING OF BANNOCKS or cakes had a particular folklore; for ritual eating, at the festival times, bannocks had to be shaped on the palm of the hand and the loose-meal from the shaping might not be put back into the meal-chest or else the Cailleach was believed to come and sit on the chest and eat up the family luck. On completion, the bannock is laid on the left palm while the right-hand thumb is turned deosil through the centre. Many heroes and heroines, setting off on their adventures, are asked by their mothers whether they will take a large bannock and no mother's blessing, or a small one and a blessing. Those who choose the latter achieve their quest, sharing their bannock with hungry strangers or animals who later help them in turn. Respect for bread, both fresh and stale, remains a strong part of domestic folklore: the woman of the house will never cast bread away unused lest want come upon her family.

TORY ISLAND, off the coast of Donegal is the traditional home of the god Balor the one-eyed, grandfather of Lugh. Balor's daughter was magically guarded on Tory, because of a prophecy that Balor would be killed by his own grandson. But Cian, Lugh's father, was able to seek out Balor's daughter, Eithne, and to lie with her, begetting Lugh. Lugh eventually returned to Tory to overcome his grandfather.

THE AES DANA were the skilled and learned class of Irish society; the title means 'the gifted people'. They might be judges, poets, craftspeople, doctors or druids. The aes dana had greater protection under law than any other people save kings. Their persons were considered immune to assault or insult, and they were treated with a respect which is still accorded in Celtic countries to all artists, skilled and gifted people today.

JUNE
15

THE ADVICE OF THE WAR-LEADER Fionn Mac Cumhail to a riotous young man:

If you aspire to adulthood, be peaceful
in the household of the powerful,
Be tough in difficult situations...
Do not be curt to common people....
Do not abandon your king while you are
in this bright world.

NAGY

JUNE
16

IN THE GAULISH CALENDRICAL TABLET, the Coligny Calendar, the month of June-July was called Equos, or 'horse-time', the season when it was possible to ride out freely in good weather and a time for horse-fairs and races.

JUNE
17

ST MOLING (D.697) founded the monastery of St Mullins in Co. Carlow, where he established the first ferry-service across the river Barrow. In true Irish fashion, he out-argued the devil who handsomely acknowledged Moling's superior nature with this endorsement:

He is pure gold, he is the sky
around the sun,
He is a vessel of silver with wine,
He is an angel, he is holy wisdom,
Whoever does the will of the King.

CM 1989

JUNE
18

WHEN CORMAC MAC ART, the Irish Solomon, was asked 'What are the three lasting things?' he replied: 'Grass, copper and yew.'

JUNE
19

MUSICAL BRANCHES of different metals were carried by the gifted people; the highest grade of the aes dana was the ollamh – roughly the equivalent to the degree of 'doctor' in modern university parlance. The ollamh bore a golden branch with bells upon it, his deputy a silver one and so on. Musical branches frequently appear as the instruments of otherworldly people, and it is thought that the poetic and druidic use of such branches was because they represented a scion of the otherworldly tree. The practical use of the musical branch was to bring attention and create silence, that people might listen more attentively to the aes dana; when in the hands of otherworldly beings, the musical branch confers a change in consciousness.

JUNE
20

ON MIDSUMMER'S EVE, young women in Ireland gathered yarrow (*Achillea millefolium*) with the rhyme:

Good morrow, good yarrow,
good morrow to thee
Send me this night my true love to see
The clothes that he'll wear,
the colour of his hair
And if he'll wed me.

DANAHER

It was placed under the pillow to induce dreams of the future beloved.

JUNE
21

MIDSUMMER is called Alban Heruin or 'the Light of the Shore' in modern druidism. This festival marks the summer solstice and the longest day. Over Midsummer, vigils, bonfires and gatherings were usual, with many people jumping through the fire to rid themselves of illness and to engender health and fertility.

JUNE
22

THE SOUTH OF IRELAND is traditionally celebrated for waterfalls, fairs, nobles, reavers, knowledge, subtlety, musicianship, melody, minstrelsy, wisdom, honour, music, learning, teaching, warriorship, fidchell playing (a chess-like board game), vehemence, fierceness, poetical art, advocacy, modesty, code, retinue, fertility.

JUNE
23

IN THE Settling of the Manor of Tara, story, Fintan proclaims that the Centre of Ireland is best known for: stewards, dignity, primacy, stability, establishments, supports, destructions, warriorship, charioteership, soldiery, principality, high-kingship, ollaveship, mead, bounty, ale, renown, great fame, prosperity.

JUNE
24

THE DRUID MOG RUITH, whose name means 'the servant of the wheel', moved through the sky upon a *roth ramach* or 'rowing wheel' which was conceived as the shining chariot of the sun. Like the sadhus of India, he performed miraculous shamanic feats, including flying through the air attired in his *encennach* or bird headdress, with magical weapons to smite his enemies. With his daughter, Tlachtga, he is a patron of wisdom and enlightenment.

Sᴛ ᴍᴏʟᴜᴀɢ (530–592) was an Irish Pict who was St Columba's rival for the island of Lismore. According to legend, Moluag cut off his thumb and cast it ashore the better to stake his claim, but Columba cursed the island. Columba was also uncomplimentary about the smallness of the enclosure about Lismore, but Moluag answered modestly that it was 'a pregnant enclosure', referring to the potential of his far-travelled missionary effort. He brought Christianity to Inverness and the Black Isle where he made another centre at Rosemarkie. His blackthorn staff, the Bachail Mor is still preserved by the Barons of the Bachail, the Livingstone clan.

Tʜᴇ ᴄʟᴀssɪᴄᴀʟ ᴡʀɪᴛᴇʀ, Diodorus Siculus, wrote of the Celtic Gauls, 'In war they carefully obey the Druids and their song-loving poets... Often times as armies approach each other in line of battle with their swords drawn and their spears raised for the charge, these men come forth between them and stop the conflict, as though they had spell-bound some kind of wild animals. Thus, even among the most savage barbarians anger yields to wisdom and Ares does homage to the Muses.' (ᴄʜᴀᴅᴡɪᴄᴋ) Celtic texts also speak of the peace-making abilities of the druids and poets.

Aᴇᴅ ꜰɪɴɴ, an Irish poet of the late Dark Ages, annotated and possibly composed *The Voyage of Maelduin*, which tells of the hero's voyage to the Blessed Islands of the Celtic Otherworld. In this episode, the travellers encounter a hermit on a tiny island: he relates his coming there and prophesies their safe return:

I cut a turf from the grey-green land of my ancestors; a sea-breeze blew me to the play I am in now, though it was compassed narrowly.

Then did the star-strong King make broad an island from the wondrous sod, of sea-gull's hue its shore line.

Each year was another foot added to the island; and best of all, a tree grew over the cresting wave.

A pure well fountained for me with eternal sustenance; by the protection of angels, sweet, food, a sacred celebration.

Each of you will come homeward, a fruitful company over the waves's track.

ᴄᴍ 1992

Cuchulainn was born Setanta, son of Dechtire and the god, Lugh. He earned his famous name by slaying the hound of Culann, in return for which, he himself became the guardian of Culann's property. He chose a short and glorious life, taking valour when only a boy. He won his wife Emer by serving the most arduous weapon-training with Scathach of Skye. His reckless behaviour in battle was due to his battle frenzy, which infected him with ecstatic disregard for the consequences: only the sight of naked women and immersion in cold tanks of water could restrain him. He is famed for his single-handed defence of Ulster during the Cattle-raid of Cooley. His slighting of the Morrighan's love brought about his death: she harried him and forced him to break his geasa.

On the feast of St Peter, fishermen consult the winds in search of a weather omen:

Wind from the west, fish and bread;
Wind from the north, cold and flaying;
Wind from the east, snow on the hills;
Wind from the south, fruit on trees.

ED. CARMICHAEL

Blodeuwedd, one of many Welsh Goddesses of Flowers, is conjured from the otherworld by Math ap Mathonwy and magically incarnated through the medium of flowers and blossoms. This is her song:

Not of mother, nor of father was my creation.
I was made from the ninefold elements:
From fruit-trees, from paradisal fruit;
From primroses and hillflowers;
From blossom of the trees and bushes;
From the roots of the earth I was made;
From the bloom of the nettle;
From water of the ninth wave.

CM 1989

The Celtic Otherworld

JULY
1

OENGUS OG, son of the Dagda and Boann, is the Irish God of Love around whose head four birds forever fluttered, representing his kisses. He himself fell in love with Caer Ibormeith who appeared to him in a dream, and his long pursuit of her became the epitomy of all lover's quests. He was the foster-father of Diarmuid O'Duibhne, lover of Grainne and transported his body to Brug na Boyne, Newgrange, after his death where he was able to breathe his soul back into his body.

JULY
2

THIS IRISH POEM by an anonymous cleric speaks of the wanderings of his distracted mind:

Sometimes along fair pathways,
  sometimes on rough roads,
on a veering course, it crosses seas
  without a ferry;
in one leap it bounds from earth to heaven;
  it runs without wisdom, hither and yon;
after lascivious travels, it comes homeward;
  neither hobble nor fetter can stay its feet,
without constancy, it never takes a rest;
  neither sword nor whiplash can restrain it,
slippery as an eel's tail sliding
  from my grasp;
locks, nor confinement,
  nor man-made chains,
strongholds nor sea, nor dark towers
  can keep it from its racing.

TRANS. CM

JULY
3

MONGAN WAS the semi-mortal son of Manannan Mac Lir and Kentigerna, queen of the Dalriadans. He was conceived by Manannan in his night-visiting aspect upon Kentigerna who received Manannan into her bed in order to prevent the death of her husband, Fiachna. Mongan was raised in the otherworld by his father and received great wisdom. Using the many skills of the trickster, Mongan tricked King Brandubh into giving back Mongan's abducted wife, Dubh-Lacha, by substituting a disguised cailleach. Many aspects of Mongan's life and conception are echoed in the folk-tale of the Great Selkie (Seal) of Sule Skerrie. He is said to be a reincarnation of Fionn Mac Cumhail.

JULY
4

THE DOG-DAYS, (3 July to 11 Aug) when Sirius rises with the sun are known as *iuchar* or the worm-month in Scots Gaelic tradition.

JULY
5

THREE FEWNESSES that are better than plenty: a fewness of fine words, a fewness of cows in pasture, a fewness of friends around good ale.

JULY
6

PELAGIUS (350–418) was a British theologian whose birth-name was Morgan: Pelagius or 'Sea-born' is a Latin equivalent of this name. He taught the doctrine that God had given humankind the innate ability of living sinlessly: a possibility that was achievable by following the example of Christ. This doctrine ran directly counter to St Augustine's doctrine that humankind was born subject to 'original sin'. As St Augustine's doctrine was the accepted orthodoxy of the Roman Church, Pelagius and his followers were subject to persecution as heretics. Nevertheless, a strong vein of Pelagianism is detectable within the Celtic Church and still surfaces from time to time where certain kinds of evangelistic Christianity have been adopted within Celtic countries.

JULY
7

ST MAELRUAIN (D.792) was the abbot of Tallaght, the most influential figure in the reforming Culdee (Celi-Dé) sect within the Irish church. The Culdees restored the full austerity of Celtic Christianity, with full enclosure, celibacy and extreme penances, in reaction to the peripetetic clergy who wandered about on pilgrimage and kept wives and children. Part of Maelruain's rule was:

Do not eat until you are hungry,
 Do not sleep until you are ready for it.
Speak to nobody without cause.

JULY
8

IN WALES, Sunday was the lucky day for marriage. A wound made with a blade that had been sharpened on a Sunday would be slow to heal: perhaps a remembrance of the making of the fatal spear which slew Lleu Llaw Gyffes, which could only be forged while mass was being said on Sunday.

JULY
9

TO DISPENSE the healing power of music was one of the many skills of the poet. Three harp-strains are said to have been instituted at the three confinements of the Goddess Boann: at her first labour, she was sorrowful because of the pain; at the second birth, she was full of joy; at the third birth she was sleepy because of the length of her labour. These three children were called Goltraiges, Gentraiges and Suantraiges, who give their names to the three strains which harpers were about to reproduce: the sorrow strain, which provokes the release of lamentation after grief; the joy strain which provokes mirth after sorrow; the sleep strain, which provokes rest after trauma.

89

JULY
10

THE VIATICUM of Llefoed Wynebglawr continues:

A city will extinguish a wilderness.
  The talkative loves easy work.
Everyone is praised according to his work.
  God loves not the hopeless.
Fortune is the best assistance.

JULY
11

IN THE IRISH TREE ALPHABET, the letter T is represented by tinne or holly.

JULY
12

THIS SLEEPING BLESSING is attributed to St Patrick:

May Thy holy angels, O Christ,
  son of the living God,
Guard our sleep, our rest, our shining bed.

Let them reveal true visions
  to us in our sleep,
O high-prince of the universe,
  O great king of the mysteries!
May no demons, no ill,
  no calamity or terrifying dreams
Disturb our rest, our willing, promote repose.

May our watch be holy, our work, our task,
  Our sleep, our rest without let,
without break.

TRANS. MEYER

JULY
13

THE SMALL ISLAND of Iona, off the Western coast of Mull in Scotland, was originally called Hy. It became the foundation of St Columba after his exile from Ireland; from Iona, the Columban missionaries went forth throughout Scotland. Although it was sacked by the Vikings, it remained an important foundation, the burial place of the Scottish kings. The abbey was restored in the early twentieth century and is now the home of the Iona Community, which is comprised of lay people. Columba's prophecy about Iona seems to have been fulfilled:

In Iona of my heart,
  Iona of my love,
Instead of monks voices
  Shall be lowing of cattle;
But ere the world come to an end,
  Iona shall be as it was.

It is also prophesied that the Second Coming of Christ as a woman shall be seen upon Iona. (MACLEOD)

THE CELTS TRADITIONALLY made offerings and prayers at wells, a custom which continues to this day, especially at those wells which have healing properties. 'Clooties' or strips of cloth are dipped in the well, prayed over and hung in the thorn tree which invariably grows over the well, there to hang and fade until the prayer, blessing or healing is achieved. All 'wishing wells' started life as primary accesses of healing power. The Struthill Well in Scotland is remembered in this wishing spell, a remnant of earlier incantations:

> *Three white stones,*
>   *And three black pins*
> *Three yellow gowans (daisies)*
>   *Off the green.*
> *Into the well,*
>   *With a one, two three,*
> *And a fortune, a fortune*
>   *Come to me.*

ED. MONTGOMERY

MEDB OR MAEVE was Queen of Connacht. She is said to have slept with or been married to many kings, although her long-term husband was Ailill. She seems to have been a priestess of the Goddess of Sovereignty, since no king was considered authentically inaugurated unless he had first slept with her. She was the cause of the Cattle Raid of Cooley, since she desired to have the Brown Bull of Cuailgne for her own herd. This brought about the conflict between Ulster and Connacht. Medb kept her beauty and youth by bathing in a certain lake, which is where she was killed. Parts of Medb's story are similar to that of the Cailleach's.

IN THE GAULISH CALENDRICAL TABLET, the Coligny Calendar, the month of July-August was called Elembiuos or 'Claim-time': during the period leading up to Lughnasadh, any unfulfilled obligations were claimed or concluded among neighbours, with legal recourse to the brehon or judge if friendly requittal were not forthcoming.

WHEN ASKED what were the three sweetest things he had ever heard, Cormac mac Airt, the Irish Solomon, replied, 'The shout of triumph after victory, praise after wages, a lady's invitation to her pillow.'

JULY
18

FIONN MAC CUMHAIL is one of the most famous of Irish heroes. After the death of his father, he was raised by two foster-mothers who taught him arms and poetry: two skills in which he remained prominent. He was apprenticed to Finneces who caught the salmon of knowledge, but received this knowledge himself by sucking his thumb after the hot fish-liquor spurted out on it. He subsequently had only to chew upon this digit when he needed supernatural knowledge of any event. He inherited the command of the fianna or royal bodyguard of the Irish High Kings, from his father. The exploits of Fionn and his fianna are the Irish equivalent of the British Arthurian legend in that a great corpus of stories, texts and songs attach to his legend.

JULY
19

CRANNCHUR OR 'casting the woods' was a druidic method of divination for judgements which was adapted to Christian use: three lots were placed in a vessel – one for guilt, one for innocence, one for the Trinity. The druid Morann mac Maine used three stones to determine guilt: a black stone for falsehood, a white stone for truth and a speckled stone for half-guilt. In each case, the accused party had to draw out one lot or stone.

JULY
20

THE QUALIFICATIONS to enter Fionn Mac Cumhail's fianna were exacting: good birth, poetic proficiency, the ability to run through the woods with no hair unbraided and no twig snapped, the ability to pull a thorn from a foot and not slacken his pace while running were included.

21

OGMA IS THE IRISH GOD of inscription and eloquence. The son of the Dagda, he invented the ogham script and is patron of its secrets. Among the continental Celts, he was called Ogmios and associated with Heracles, being depicted as a bald, old man. The Greek writer, Lucian of Samosata, describes Ogmios as leading a happy band of men behind him, attached to his tongue by golden chains fixed to their ears. This image may be associated with the Plutarchian image of a semi-divine race who inhabit the happy otherworldly island of Ogygia. 'In one of these islands... Cronus is confined by Zeus and the antique Briareus... (here) Heracles has the highest honours.' Plutarch goes on to tell how every thirty years when Saturn (called among the British, the Night-watchman) enters Taurus, a party of voyagers go forth to Ogygia to learn the sacred arts. The interrelationship of Ogmios with Heracles is because the Celts associated eloquence with strength. (PLUTARCH)

In the poems of Taliesin, Heracles is frequently referenced.

22

THE STARS of the directions are addressed in this Gaelic prayer:

Star of the East, give us kingly birth;
Star of the South, give us great love;
Star of the West, give us quiet age;
Star of the North, give us death.

MACLEOD

23

THREE THINGS which strength custom: fairness, power and authority. Three things which weaken custom: oppression, doubtful origin and bad example.

24

AMONG THE INNER HEBRIDES, it was the custom for a newborn child to be taken by its mother outside and, at noon and in the sun, to touch the baby's brow to the ground. This was called 'the old Mothering'. 'How could one better be blessed, on coming into life, than to have the kiss of that ancient Mother of whom we are all children?' (MACLEOD)

25

IN THE IRISH TREE ALPHABET, the letter CW or Q is represented by quert or apple. In Celtic tradition, the apple is always regarded as a blessed fruit, in contradiction to the Classical myth of the apple of discord, or the late Christian association of the apple with the forbidden fruit of the Edenic Tree. In the Voyage of Maelduin, the apple is the fruit which nurtures and sustains life; in the lore of Avalon, it is the fruit which heals and restores. The sound 'cw' is absent from Brythonic Celtic languages and is replaced by 'p' as is readily seen by comparing the Gaelic and British words for 'Pict' – Cruitne and Priteni.

93

26

THE SUNDAY BEFORE LUGHNASADH is called Height Sunday in Ireland, when many people make pilgrimage to the mountains and high places. This ancient custom may be motivated by the need to ascend to the highest place in order to see the dispositions of the land at this season and to intercede with the gods of harvest. Many such pilgrimages are still performed, the most notable being the ascent of Croagh Patrick in County Mayo.

The Life of St Patrick says that God had commanded the saints of Ireland, 'go up above the mountain which towers and is higher than all the mountains that are towards the setting of the sun, to bless the people of Ireland, that Patrick might see the fruit of his labour.' Pilgrims still make the climb, usually on bare feet and fasting, stopping at designated stations on the way up to recite prayers and going on to celebrate mass at the summit.

94

27

THIS POEM, ascribed to Rumann, a poet who died in 748, speaks of a storm at sea and incorporates some of the ancient Celtic teachings about the winds:

> When the wind blows from the east,
>   Then stirs the spirit of the wave;
> It longs to go westwards, beyond us,
>   To the land of the sun's sleeping,
> To the blue ocean's vast billow.
>
> When the wind blows from the north,
>   The dark ravening wave sweeps down;
> It longs to battle the southern world,
>   To struggle against the wide skies,
> To listen to the swan's music.
>
> When the wind blows from the west,
>   Over the swift sea currents;
> It longs to roll eastwards, beyond us,
>   To seize the Sun-Tree,
> In the wide, distant seas.
>
> When the wind strikes from the south,
>   Over the shield-bearing Saxonlands;
> It mingles with the wave of Skiddy Island,
>   It drenches the summit of Calad Nit
> With a blue-grey weedy mantle.

TRANS. CM

28

ST SAMSON (D.565), bishop of Dol in Brittany, is associated chiefly with the areas of his missionary work, namely in Cornwall, Scilly, Wales and the Channel Islands. His miraculous conception by Anna of Gwent seems to be rooted in an ancient propitiatory custom: a wise man advised his father, Amon of Demetia, to make a silver rod as tall as Anna and give it as alms to the poor. Amon made three such rods and Samson was conceived. The giving of precious metal rods was a legal requirement if a king's honour had been violated. In the laws of Hywel Dda, the *sarhad* or honour-price of a king had to be compensated by considerable gifts. The ritual of Samson's conception is therefore a method of sacred redemption comparable to the Hebrew custom of redeeming first-born children with the sacrifice of a lamb or dove, as Christ's mother and foster-father do at Candlemas. Samson is accounted by Alan de Insulis as one of the Seven Saints of Britain.

29

AINE, THE IRISH GODDESS of health, was worshipped around County Limerick at Cnoc Aine. She was responsible for the vital spark of life which was believed to circulate around the entire body every twenty four hours. No healers would practice bloodletting on this day, as they believed that the vital spark would flow away (CM 1994).

The cult of Aine continued into the Middle Ages, when it was said that Maurice, first Earl of Desmond (D.1356) and Aine had a son, Gearóid Iarla, the historical third Earl of Desmond (1359–98) who was also a poet.

30

BALOR WAS THE FOMORIAN GOD of sorcery. He had only one eye, the other having been scorched by viewing the preparation of a druidic cauldron of knowledge. Balor cast his daughter's child, Lugh into the sea, but he was saved by the seals and fostered by the smith-god, Goibhniu. He grew to become Lugh Lamhfada, the Long-Armed. At the Second Battle of Mag Tuiread, Lugh defeated Balor, as prophesied, by casting a stone shot into his eye and thus diminishing the magical power of the Fomorian people.

31

JULY WAS OFTEN CALLED 'the hungry month' due to the fact that, before harvest, people often faced famine, having run through their supplies since the previous harvest. It was for this reason that they looked forward so keenly to Lughnasadh for, as the saying went, 'tomorrow is Lughnasadh Day when all fruits ripen'. (MACNEIL)

The festival of Lughnasadh now begins, when all gather together in friendship and common interest to gather in the grain and celebrate the harvest of the year.

LUGHNASADH

AUTUMN'S BOUNTY

The grain stands tall in the fields, the days are misty and hot as we gather the harvest of the year. Lughnasadh sees three harvests: the grain harvest of August, the fruit harvest of September and the meat harvest of October – November when beasts are slaughtered for Winter-eating. There is plenty in the larder and a feeling of unaccustomed richness. As Autumn progresses, animals make their own harvest of the year's plenty against the dark days of Winter, gathering fruits and nuts.

The season of Lughnasadh is one of transition when we adjust to the lessening of heat and of assimilation as we assess the harvest of our work while the leaves fall.

Culhwch Sets Out on Quest

LUGHNASADH OPENS the last quarter of the Celtic year. The festival derives from the funeral games held by the Irish god, Lugh, in honour of his foster-mother Tailtiu, and its name means 'the binding duty of Lugh'. Tailtiu was an ancient goddess of agriculture who is said to have died from having cleared the plains of trees ready for planting: since this clearing of the Irish forests took place in earliest times, we may conclude that Tailtiu is a Gaelic name for an even more ancient goddess. Lugh, son of Ethniu, is also called Samildanach, or 'he of the many gifts', since there was no skill or art to which he was a stranger. It is fitting that his name should be given to this feast which celebrates the harvest of all the fruits of the earth. Indeed, in Ireland, people looked forward anxiously to this time when, instead of surviving on the remnants of last year's harvest, they would 'be on the pig's back' with plenty. Lughnasadh covered the harvest months when all people were in the fields to help bring in the grain. Two great fairs were held at this time in ancient Ireland one of which, the Oenach Tailten, survived until the late eighteenth century at Teltown, Co. Meath. One of the customs of this fair was that of the 'Teltown marriage', whereby a wall was erected in which was a hole big enough to admit a hand. Men and women stood on either side of the hole and whoever grasped the other's hand through it were considered married for nine months: if either party were dissatisfied at the end of which time, the trial marriage was cancelled. Marriages were common after harvest-time, since small-holders could establish whether they could afford to get married in the coming year, although in rural Ireland, getting wed during the harvest was generally avoided as unlucky. The sacrifice of a bull seems associated with this festival, possibly to feed the assemblies which gathered to celebrate the harvest. Many games and contests were part of these celebrations, including the swimming of horses across lakes, contests of strength, dancing and skill.

This festival marks a deeper awareness of the marriage between the land and its people. Lugh frequently appears in vision to aid and assist candidate kings in their quest for kingship; in his hall sits the Goddess of Sovereignty who dispenses the red drink of lordship to the worthy candidate.

WHEN LUGH and the Tuatha de Danaan were victorious over the Fomorians, they captured the Fomorian king, Bres, and promised to spare his life if he granted his gifts of agriculture to them. First Bres offered a continual supply of milk, then a harvest in each season: these gifts were rejected because they broke the natural order of things. The Tuatha de Danaan replied:

This has been our way:
  Spring for ploughing and sowing,
Summer for strengthening
  and encouraging the grain,
Autumn for ripening the corn and reaping it,
  Winter for enjoying it.

MACNEIL

But they accepted his advice on ploughing, sowing and reaping, and so it is that the blessing of 'corn and milk in your land and mast in your woods and increase in your soil' is maintained to this day.

3

THE FIRST SUNDAY in August was the time of pilgrimage to the Llyn a Fan Fach near Llanddeusant in Dyfed. Here in the twelfth century, a boy met a faery woman issuing from this lake and married her. Their union was dependent upon his behaviour: if he hit her three times, she would leave him. Although he vowed to maintain his promise, he was driven to hitting her twice because she laughed at a funeral and cried at a wedding. The last blow was an accident, at which she returned to the lake. She returned once to give her children herbal wisdom which they wrote down. Their lineage, called the Physicians of Myddfai, descends to this day.

4

CULHWCH WAS CURSED with hopeless love for Olwen, a giant's daughter, by his stepmother. In his headlong pursuit of Olwen, Culhwch had to overcome thirty-nine impossible tasks set by Ysbaddaden, her father. These he achieved with the help of his uncle, King Arthur. These tasks included finding the lost child Mabon, overcoming enchantments and securing the comb and scissors that were tied between the ears of the ferocious boar, Twrch Trwyth.

5

THREE KEYS that unlock thoughts: drunkenness, trustfulness, love.

6

THE BEHAVIOUR of Celtic kings was believed to affect the nature of the land and weather: 'By the Prince's Truth fair weather comes in each fitting season, winter fine and frosty, spring dry and windy, summer warm with showers of rain, autumn with heavy dews and fruitful. For it is the prince's falsehood that bring perverse weather upon wicked peoples and dries up the fruit of the earth.' (BYRNE)

7

ONE OF THE WONDERS that Nennius enumerates in his Wonders of Wales, is a heap of stones in Builth. On this is the footprint of Arthur's hound, Cabal, which was impressed upon it when they were hunting for the boar Twrch Trwyth.

THE NUMBER THREE is the sacred number of the Celts. Triadic sayings are common to all Celtic countries and these are undoubtedly remnants of ancient druidic teachings: they remain concise encapsulizations of ancient memory. The triple spiral or triskel is the basis for much Celtic ornament and is a central symbol for the three-fold nature of the soul. Three elements are frequently invoked as witnesses to oaths: earth, sea and sky.

DIARMUID UA DUIBHNE was fostered by Oengus mac Og and was famed for his love-spot which made women speedily fall in love with him. Diarmuid was a prominent member of the fianna, accompanying Fionn on many adventures. He fell out with Fionn Mac Cumhail when Fionn married Gráinne: Gráinne was appalled at having to marry an elderly warrior, however famous, and chose to elope with Diarmuid instead. They spent sixteen years in the wild, never staying in one place for two nights together, so that many megalithic stones and monuments throughout Ireland are called 'the beds of Diarmuid and Gráinne'. (These were much frequented by couples desirous of fertility.) After pursuing them for many years, Fionn finally relented. At his birth, Diarmuid's stepbrother's soul had been sent into the form of a boar which was destined to kill Diarmuid. Finally, Diarmuid attempted to kill this same boar and was fatally wounded by it. In his death-agony, Diarmuid appealed to Fionn's healing but Fionn was unable to comply, still wracked with jealousy and shame over Diarmuid's abduction of Gráinne.

MYRDDIN EMRYS or Merlin is the traditional keeper of Britain, one of whose names was Clas Myrddin, or Merlin's Enclosure. He is better known as the druidic adviser and prophet of Arthur, although he prepares the coming of the Pendragon line by exposing the treacherous king, Vortigern. He retires to his otherworldly observatory of seventy-two doors and windows (the sacred nine times eight) at the end of his career, the better to keep watch on the doings of Britain.

AUGUST
11

THE FAERY HOSTS of the Sidhe or Place of Peace are described in this anonymous Irish poem:

White shields they carry in their hands,
* With emblems of pale silver;*
With glittering blue swords,
* With mighty stout horns....*

With smooth comely bodies,
* With bright blue-starred eyes,*
With pure crystal teeth,
* With thin red lips.*

Good they are at man-slaying,
* Melodious in the ale-house,*
Masterly at making songs,
* Skilled at playing fidhchell.*

TRANS. MEYER

AUGUST
12

THREE RENEWINGS of the world: a woman's womb, a cow's udder, a smith's fire.

AUGUST
13

YNYS WITRIN or Glastonbury, is no longer an island unless heavy rains sweep the Somerset levels, but its old title, meaning the Island of Glass, is a remembrance of its otherworldly connections. The Tor is the gateway to the realm of Gwyn ap Nudd.

AUGUST
14

WHEN ASKED about his behaviour as child, Cormac mac Airt replied:

I was a listener in woods,
* I was a gazer at stars,*
I was blind where secrets were concerned,
* I was silent in a wilderness,*
I was talkative among many,
* I was mild in the mead-hall,*
I was stern in battle,
* I was gentle towards allies,*
I was a physician to the sick ...
* I did not deride the old though I was young...*
I would not speak about
* anyone in his absence.*

TRANS. MEYER

AUGUST
15

IN THE WESTERN HIGHLANDS of Scotland, the Assumption of the Virgin was celebrated by the making of a sacred bannock, cooked over rowan wood. As each member of the family ate some, they raised the Praise-Song of the Mother, walking deosil around the fire:

I go deosil around my dwelling,
* In the name of our Mother Mary,*
Who promised to preserve me,
* Who preserves me,*
Who will preserve me,
* In peace, in flocks,*
In trueness of heart,
* In work, in love,*
In wisdom, in mercy.

TRANS. CM

IN THE GAULISH CALENDRICAL TABLET, the Coligny Calendar, the month of August-September was called Edrinios or 'arbitration time', since the period after harvest was a suitable time of assembly when disputes could be legally settled satisfactorily.

MANY IRISH STORIES tell of heroes who make wonder voyages to the Celtic otherworld. The aim of many of these voyages is to discover the fabled Land of Women, where faery women dwell together in blissful harmony. The voyager, Maéldiun, makes the landfall upon this island and finds perfect happiness as the consort of the Queen of the Land of Women. When his crew grow discontented with otherworldly existence and seek to return home, they have difficulty persuading Maelduin to accompany them, so completely enthralled is their captain with the Queen.

THE OATH OF UGAINE MÓR, (6TH CENTURY BC), High King of Ireland, establishing the right of his descendants to reign at Tara was sworn 'by the sun and moon and sea and dew and light and by all the elements visible and invisible and every element in heaven and on earth.' Ugaine's power was so great that he took hostages not only in Ireland and Scotland, but also in Brittany as well. It was he who divided Ireland into twenty-five parts among his children. This number recurs in the twenty-five battalions of the High King's fianna.

THREE BEST THINGS for a king: merit, peace and an army.

104

A KING WHO REFUSED the proper reward for a poem was likely to have the *glam dicind* performed against him: this was a ritual satire with terrible effect. After fasting against the king, the poet with six poets of each degree went to a hilltop. Facing the king against whom the satire was directed, with their backs to a hawthorn, with the wind from the north, and in each man's hand a slingstone and hawthorn thorn; each sung a verse into the slingstone and placed them under the hawthorn. If the satire were unjust, the earth would swallow the poets up; but if the king were in the wrong then the king, his wife, son, horse, arms, clothes and hound would be swallowed up by the earth. Many lesser satires were practised by aggrieved poets, causing facial blemishes or other misfortunes. The power of the word spoken with intent was the chief skill of the poets, one which was subject to abuse. Such was the fear of such magical retaliation and excessive poetic demands on their patrons, that the Convention of Drum Ceatt in 575 was called to limit poetic powers.

T HIS BLESSING against the jealousy of others comes from the Scottish Highlands:

Power of wind is mine over it,
  Power of anger is mine over it,
Power of fire is mine over it,
  Power of thunder is mine over it,
Power of lightning is mine over it,
  Power of storm is mine over it,
Power of moon is mine over it,
  Power of sun is mine over it,
Power of stars is mine over it,
  Power of sky is mine over it,
Power of heavens
  And of the worlds is mine over it.

A share upon the grey rocks,
  A share upon the steep hills,
A share upon the fast falls,
  A share upon the wide fields,
And a share upon the mighty salt sea,
  For she is best to disperse its ill.

In the name of the life-giving Threefold,
  In the name of the Sacred Three,
In the name of all the Secret Ones,
  And of all the Powers.

TRANS. CM

IN THE IRISH TREE ALPHABET, the letter M is represented by muin or blackberry which is about to fruit at this time.

LUGHNASADH IS THE TIME of the inauguration of kings. The Celtic rites of sovereignty were performed on hills where the candidate, chosen from the ranks of the royal kindred, would be raised up in front of the clan and acclaimed, often by setting his foot into the ancestral footprint in the rock, as at Dunadd in Argyll, or by sitting upon an inauguration stone, like the Stone of Scone.

THREE PLACES ARE MY BEST-BELOVED in the peopled world: Durrow; Derry, that noble angelic city; and Tir Luigdech. But, if the King of the Sun and the Angels permitted me, I should choose Gartan to be my burial place above any other three in the world.

(TRANS. CM)

ST MAELRUBHA (642–722) was an apostle to the Picts of Ross and Cromarty. A descendant of King Niall of the Nine Hostages, on his father's side and of a Pictish mother, he chose to leave Ireland and suffer the 'white martyrdom' of exile on his missions. His saint's day was celebrated as late as 1678, when bulls were still being sacrificed to Mourie, a pre-Christian deity with whom he became fused.

DICHETUL DO CHENNAIB or psychometric divination was one of the Three Illuminations or prophetic skills required of an ollamh of poetry in Ireland. By placing his hands or a wand upon a person or object, he gained knowledge through his fingers and could name and tell the history of that person or object.

THIS SCOTS GAELIC HEALING CHARM, disperses the illness to the vastation of the elements by means of their animal inhabitants:

Since you are the King of all goodness,
  Since you are the King of Heaven,
I pray that you lift each wasting,
  Each weariness and weakness,
Each seizure and illness,
  Each soreness and discomfort,
Each malady and sickness
  That afflicts _____.
(the sick person's name)

May it go with the beasts of the heights,
  May it go with the wild ones
  of the wilderness,
May it go with the winged ones
of the summits,
  May it go with the whales of the seas,
May it go with the streams of the glens,
  May it go with the whales of the seas,
May it go with the crests of the bens,
  May it go with the birds of the air.

May the God of guidance
  scatter this day/night,
every ill and affliction
  that abides in your flesh!

TRANS. CM

ANDRASTE WAS THE BRITISH GOD-DESS of Victory to whom Queen Boudicca of the Iceni sacrificed in her campaign against the injustices of the Roman regime. Before setting out on campaign, Boudicca released a hare, sacred to Andraste, from her cloak in order to divine the outcome by the hare's track.

IN THE LUDICROUS IRISH TALE of *The Great Visitation to Guaire*, the swine-herd, Marban, entered into a contest with the poets lodged at Guaire's house. Dael Duiled, the chief poet of Leinster, asked him these riddles: 'what good thing did Man find on earth that God did not find? Which are the two trees whose foliage does not fall till they die? What beast lives in the sea and is drowned when it is taken out of it? What animal lives in fire and is burnt when it is taken out?' Marban correctly gave the respective answers: 'a worthy man; the holly and the yew; the Gním Abraein (an unidentified animal); and the Tegillus or Salamander. Marban overcame all the poets and set a geas upon them to recite the story of the Cattle Raid of Cooley, and, since none could, not to rest two nights in one place until they had discovered the story. It was only by raising Fergus mac Roich from the grave, that the poets were able to regain their honour and comply with Marban's request.

(DILLON)

ACCORDING TO THE LAWS of Hywel Dda, there are 'three arts which a bondman cannot teach his son without the consent of his lord: clerkship, smithcraft and bardism; for if the lord be passive until the clerk be tonsured, or until the smith enter his smithy, or until a bard graduate, he can never enslave them after that. (RICHARDS)

ST AIDAN (D.651) was a monk of Iona who founded the monastery of Lindisfarne and became the Celtic apostle to the Northumbrian Anglo-Saxons. He advocated simplicity in teaching and common sense and compassion in his daily dealings. His example alone caused him to be revered by many noble and wealthy families, though he always used their gifts to relieve suffering and redeem slaves, even giving away the horse given him by King Oswin because he preferred to be on the same level as ordinary folk.

The Spirits of Baile and Ailenn Embrace

1

THIS RHYME on how to sain or bless a corpse comes from Scotland; vernacular expressions are translated in brackets:

> Thrice the torchie, thrice the saltie,
>   Thrice the dishes toom for loffie –
>   (empty for bread)
> These three times ye must wave round
>   The corpse, till it sleep sound.
> Sleep sound and frown nane
>   Till to heaven the souls gane.
> If you want that soul to diè,
>   Procure the torchie frae Elleręe. (seer)
> But gin ye want the soul to live,
>   Between the dishes place a sieve
> And it shall have a fair,
>   fair shrive (absolution from sin).

2

THIS SONG OF THE SOUL from the Black Book of Carmarthan speaks of the nature of the soul before birth:

> It was with seven faculties that
>   I was thus blessed,
> With seven created beings
>   I was placed for purification;
> I was gleaming fire when
>   I was caused to exist;
> I was dust of the earth,
>   and grief could not reach me;
> I was a high wind,
>   being less evil than good;
> I was a mist on a mountain
>   seeking supplies of stags;
> I was blossoms of trees
>   on the face of the earth.
> If the Lord had blessed me,
>   He would have placed me on matter.
> Soul, such was I made.

ED. SKENE

3

BAILE AND AILINN were lovers who had been parted. On hearing false report of each other's deaths, they each died and were buried in separate graves. Out of Baile's grave grew a yew, out of Ailinn's an apple. After some years, poets and seers cut down the yew to create a poet's tablet relating the vision-tales, feasts, loves and wooings of Ulster. Similarly, in Leinster, the poets made a poet's tablet out of the apple tree relating comparable tales from Leinster. At the Samhain feast held by Art mac Conn, both ranks of regional poets assembled, bring their tablets with them. The two tablets sprang together, inseparable as woodbine about a branch. The unified wood from the lover's graves was kept in the treasury of Tara as a wonder.

4

RHIANNON IS THE RESOURCEFUL HEROINE of the story, *Pwyll, Prince of Dyfed*. A Goddess of the Underworld, she chose a mortal condition in order to marry Pwyll and overturned her father's desire for her to marry Gwawl, a disruptive Underworld being whose malice caused him to steal Rhiannon's newborn son. Since the midwives attendant on her feared Pwyll's anger, they smeared dog's blood on Rhiannon's face and cast dog-bones about the bed to set the blame of the child's disappearance upon her. For seven years, Rhiannon was sentenced to stand at the mounting block, to stop all strangers and tell them this tale against herself and then offer her own back to carry them into the hall. After a few years, her son was restored to her and she was exonerated from blame. After Pwyll's death, she married Manawyddan ap Llyr and was again subject to otherworldly enchantment. Her three blackbirds grant forgetfulness, delight and refreshment.

5

THREE CANDLES that illume every darkness: truth, nature, knowledge.

6

SUIBHNE, THE SON of a Dalriadan king, was so irritated by the church bell of St Ronan, that he rushed naked out the house and threw Ronan's psalter into a lake. Ronan cursed Suibhne with the curse of wandering as naked through the world as he had done by coming naked into the saint's presence. Suibhne was stricken with a flying madness thereafter. He eventually took shelter near the monastery of St Moling where he was slain by the cook who believed Suibhne to be sleeping with the cook's wife. Before he died, Suibhne sang:

Sweeter to me once than the sound of a bell beside me was the song of a blackbird on the mountain and the belling of the stag in a storm.

Sweeter to me once than the voice of a lovely woman beside me was the voice of the mountain grouse at dawn.

Sweeter to me once was the cry of wolves than the voice of a cleric within, bleating and whining.

TRANS. DILLON

7

IN THE IRISH TREE ALPHABET, the letter G is represented by gort or ivy.

8

THE NUMBER NINE is prominant in Celtic lore, composed of the sacred three, times three. Nine waves demark the sovereignty of any coast-line and to go beyond nine waves indicates exile; nine maidens kindle the cauldron of the Underworld; the Beltane fire was kindled with nine sticks from nine different trees and lit by nine men.

109

110

9

LOCH LOCHAIDH near Lochaber in Scotland was called the lake of the Black Goddess in ancient times; it was still venerated under this name when St Columba was missionizing the area. The Black Goddess is another name for the Cailleach.

10

ST FINNIAN OF MOVILLE (D.579) was educated at St Ninian's monastery at Whithorn and founded Moville in 550. His most famous pupil was St Columba who was responsible for secretly copying Finnian's beautiful psalter. When Finnian discovered what had happened, he insisted that the copy legally belonged to himself, not to Columba. In one of the earliest copyright cases, King Diarmuid mac Cerbaill judged, 'to every cow her calf, to every book its little book', so that Columba had to ignominiously return the psalter he had so painstakingly copied from Finnian's scriptorium.

11

CORMAC MAC ART was recognized as High King when he came, incognito to Tara. He found a woman weeping and asked the steward who was consoling her what ailed her. 'The King judges that her sheep are forfeit for having stripped the queen's woad-garden bare.' 'It would be more fitting for one shearing of the woman's wool to pay for one shearing of the woad garden. Surely, the man who passed that judgement never made a false judgement before this,' said Cormac. The steward brought word of this to King Art mac Conn, who immediately recognized that Cormac indeed must be his own son and that his own term of kingship must be at an end. (DILLON)

12

THREE THINGS WHICH A KING does not share with anyone: his treasure, his hawk and his thief (taxman).

13

EMAIN ABHLACH, the Isle of Apples, is the old name for the island of Arran in Scotland, the abode of Manannan mac Lir, God of the Sea and of the Otherworld. This realm has the same reputation as that of Avalon, in that it is pleasant land where the weather is always clement and where snow never falls.

14

MABSANT WAS A FESTIVAL held in Wales at nutting time, usually coinciding with the Christian feast of Holy Cross Day, which commemorates the finding of the Cross by St Helena. The nut-gatherers returned to the inn where they played games, using the nuts to pay fines and forfeits. Mabsant was a name generally given to the locality's patron saint, in whose honour dances and assemblies were held. Musicians travelled from Mabsant to Mabsant around the land. One Glamorgan harpist began such a circuit when he was twenty-three and retired when he was eighty-three!

15

IN THE GAULISH calendrical tablet, the Coligny Calendar, the month of September-October was called Cantlos or 'song-time', since this was the season when the agricultural year was winding down and the delights of winter leisure were beginning. At this season, wandering bards would seek patrons to accommodate and feed them over the winter.

16

ST NINIAN (5TH CENTURY) was the principle apostle to the southern Picts. Ninian was greatly inspired by the monasticism of St Martin of Tours and founded his monastery, called the White House at Whithorn, possibly enshrining there a relic of St Martin. Ninian's reputation for healing long-standing diseases made Whithorn a place of pilgrimage. St Ailred of Rievaulx called him ' a light upon a candlestick', and tells of how Ninian healed King Tudwal of a blindness that was both physical and spiritual.

17

NINE-FOLD GROUPS of dedicated women act as inspirers, foster-mothers and teachers, their blessing maintaining the sacred order in the Celtic world. Sometimes called 'the nine witches', their function is a sacral one, for they act as the maintainers of the sacred flame, they initiate children into knowledge and, as the nine guardians of the Cauldron of Annwn, are the original faery godmothers who imbue each living soul with innate gifts.

(C & J MATTHEWS 1993)

111

18

ROSMERTA WAS A GODDESS venerated as 'the Great Provider'. She appears most often carrying a Classical cornucopia or offering dish. In Romano-Celtic dedications she is most often paired with the Roman god, Mercury, although she also appears as a Goddess of Plenty.

19

THE FAERY KIND are said to possess nine ages – nine times nine periods of time make up each age:

Nine nines sucking the breast.
 Nine nines unsteady, weak,
Nine nines on foot, swift,
 Nine nines able and strong,
Nine nines strapping, brown,
 Nine nines victorious, subduing,
Nine nines bonneted, drab,
 Nine nines beardy, grey.
Nine nines on the breast-beating death,
 And worse to me were
 these miserable nine nines
Than all the other short-lived
nine nines that were.

C & J MATTHEWS 1993

20

DEIRDRIU WAS THE DAUGHTER of Felimidh. While yet in her mother's womb, she uttered a terrible shriek which the druid Cathbad interpreted as a prophecy of sorrow. He predicted that through her great misfortune would come, but Conchobor sought to avert this by raising her in isolation from men in order to marry her himself. As a young woman, Deirdriu had a vision of the man she would love by looking at a raven stooping on some blood in the snow: she wished for one whose hair was as black, whose skin was as white, whose lips were as red as this vision. Her eye fell upon Naoisi, one of the Sons of Usnech. Together with him and his brothers, she escaped the wrath of Conchobor by fleeing to Scotland where they lived for many years. Eventually, Conchobor tricked the honourable Fergus mac Roich, into guaranteeing the safe-return of the exiles, upon which he had the Sons of Usnech slain. Deirdriu committed suicide rather than live without her lover. A portion of her great lament follows:

Ulster's high-king, my first husband,
I forsook for Naoisi's love;
Short my life after them,
I will perform their funeral game.

After them I will not be alive –
Three that would go into every conflict,
Three who liked to endure hardships,
Three heroes who never refused combat.

O man that diggest the tomb,
And that puttest my darling from me,
Make not the grave too narrow,
I shall be beside the noble ones.

TRANS. MEYER

21

THE AUTUMN EQUINOX is called Alban Elued or 'the Light of the Water' among the reformed druidic orders. This day represents the sun's mid-way point between midsummer and midwinter and so 'the light of the water' indicates the descent of the sun into the cosmic ocean. As Lughnasadh marks the grain-harvest, so this festival marks the fruit harvest.

22

THE WEST OF IRELAND is traditionally known for: learning, foundation, teaching, alliance, judgement, chronicles, counsels, stories, histories, sciences, comeliness, eloquence, beauty, modesty, bounty, abundance and wealth.

23

ST ADAMNAN (627–704) was born in Donegal and became a monk at Iona. On a visit to Ceolfrith of Wearmouth, he became convinced of the Roman method of dating Easter and returned to Ireland as the major exponent of the Roman school: as the result of this most Irish churches began to celebrate Easter in common with Rome, except for Iona and its daughter missions which held out for the Celtic method. Adamnan wrote the *Cain Adomnain* which protected women, boys and clerics from military service: a rule which was accepted throughout Ireland. He was the chief biographer of St Columba.

24

THREE ANIMALS whose acts towards unwise men are not recognized in law: a stallion while seeking mares in heat; a bull which is seeking cows in heat from the calends of May to the calends of winter; and a boar while the swine of his herd are brimming. No compensation is made for anything these animals may do to one who unwisely intervenes.

SEPTEMBER
25

𝕿HIS BLESSING WAS MADE upon the Eoghanacht kings of Cashel, Munster:

> *Blessing of heaven – cloud blessing,*
> *blessing of earth – fruit blessing,*
> *blessing of sea – fish blessing,*
> *blessing of sun – rank blessing,*
> *blessing of moon – honour blessing,*
> *blessing of ale – food blessing,*
> *blessing of light – dew blessing,*
> *blessing of wisdom – valour blessing,*
> *blessing of grain – plough blessing.*
>
> BYRNE

SEPTEMBER
26

𝕹ELDORACHT WAS A DRUIDIC METHOD OF DIVINATION often involving cloud-watching or star-gazing. We know that this method was used in the creation of the Coligny Calendar, since each night is annotated with remarks about the clarity or cloudiness of the heavens and the subsequent omens which accompany each day.

SEPTEMBER
27

𝕱ERGUS MAC ROITH was one of the senior warriors of the Red Branch Host of Ulster. His honour was treacherously entailed by Conchobor, who used him to entice Deirdriu and the Sons of Usnach home from their exile in Alba, as a result of which, Fergus went into exile in Connacht. He has the reputation of the most virile men. The stone at Tara was called 'the phallus of Fergus'.

THE DANCE called *Cailleach An Dudean*, the Hag of the Mill-dust, was performed on Michaelmas eve in the Western Highlands of Scotland. The man held a rod, called the Slachdan Druiheachd, the druid's wand, which he held over his own head and then over the woman who then fell down, as if dead. He danced in mourning, then touched each of her limbs in order until each came to life, then he knelt and breathed into her mouth and touched her heart with the wand to raise her up again. She then danced joyously with her partner.

RIDING THE STANG was the traditional Scottish punishment inflicted on wife-beaters by the community: the culprit was made to sit astride a fir-pole whose stumps had been pruned down to the length of an inch. The crowd would chorus:

> *Ocht yt's richt'll (All that's right will)*
> *   no be wrang:*
> *Lik (Beat) the wife and ride the Stang.*

As they chorused 'Stang', the fir-pole would be lifted high and suddenly let down again so that the culprit would be scratched by the ends of the branches during this salutary punishment.

THE CUSTOM OF CUTTING the last sheaf of grain or the Cailleach's Sheaf was practised all over the Celtic world. In Shropshire, this custom is called 'Cutting the Neck' or 'Crying the Mare', where the last standing bunches of grain were tied up like mare's legs and the reapers took turns at throwing their sickles to sever the last sheaf. In Wales, this custom was called 'Y Gaseg Fedi', the Harvest Mare. No-one would willingly be selected for this ritual since it carried overtones of ill-luck and sacrifice, so that all the harvesters would try throwing their sickles at one time so that no individual was marked out. The last sheaf was often brought in and made into a corn-dolly to be venerated as the power of the fields until the next year.

The Goddess of Sovereignty

1

THE FRITH OR AUGURY was practised in the Western Highlands of Scotland. The seer, fasting, bare-foot and with closed eyes, took an augury of the coming season by standing upon the threshold on the first day of the quarter, with one hand upon either door-jamb. When she opened her eyes she took her augury from what kinds of animals met her gaze: their colour, movement and kind foretold the *frith*.

2

THREE ONE-FOOTED ANIMALS: a horse, a greyhound and a hawk: whoso wounds but one foot of them must pay their full worth.

3

THIS SONG, *Chi Mi Na Morbheanna*, was composed by John Cameron of Ballachulish in 1856; it recalls the homecoming of the exile and so is often sung or played at the funerals of ex-patriot Gaels, as it was at the funeral of John F. Kennedy in 1963. The tune was incorporated into the score of the feature film, Local Hero by Mark Knopfler.

See, O see, the mighty mountain!
See, O see, the lofty benn!
See, O see, the rugged corries!
Under the mist the peaks I see!

Before me I see the place of birth,
Welcomed I will be in a tongue that I know,
Love and hospitality will be offered me,
That I would not trade for tons of gold.

I see the woods, I see the thickets,
I see the fair and fruitful fields,
I see the deer grazing the corries,
Shrouded in a robe of mist.

Mountains high with lovely slopes,
The folk abiding there with kindly hearts;
Light my step as I bound towards them,
And willingly will I bide there a while.

TRANS. CM

4

PWYLL, PRINCE OF DYFED, had his court at Arberth. He encountered the hounds of Arawn, Lord of the Underworld, while out hunting and attempted to drive them off the stag which he was pursuing himself. Arawn appeared to ask for compensation for this insult. Pwyll agreed to go in the shape of Arawn for a year and defend his kingdom, while Arawn took Pwyll's shape and changed places with him. As a mortal, Pwyll is able to overcome Arawn's enemy Hafgan. After the year is up, they change places again and Pwyll accepts a gift of otherworldly pigs, the first ever seen, and the title of 'Lord of Annwn'. Ascending the mound at Arberth, Pwyll encounters Rhiannon and sets out to marry her against supernatural odds, including the treacherous retaliation of her former suitor, Gwawl, whom he eventually overcomes with the help of Rhiannon's resourcefulness. Although forced to judge his wife for the alleged cannibalization of their son, Pwyll, does not slay her but gives her a seven-year punishment.

117

THREE COFFERS whose depths is not known: the coffers of a chieftain, the coffers of the Church, the coffers of a privileged poet.

WHAT IS IT?

In comes two legs, carrying one leg,
Lays down one leg, on three legs,
Out goes two legs, in comes four legs,
Out goes five legs, in comes two legs,
Snatches up three legs, flings it at four legs,
And brings back one leg.

Answer – A woman bringing in a leg of mutton which she places on a stool; she goes out and a dog comes and runs off with the meat; the woman returns, throws the stool at the dog and brings back the mutton-leg.

IN THE IRISH TREE ALPHABET, the letter NG is represented by ngetal or reed.

The number five is a unit of family and implicit order in Ireland which was and is still divided into five provinces, despite the political partition of Northern Ireland as a British state. There were five laws and prohibitions upon Ireland's provincial kings; the ogam tree alphabet is grouped in families of five; the breath of a poet was believed to be five words long.

THE WATERS OF SUL, called by the Romans Aquae Sulis, are the only hot water springs in Britain. This sacred Celtic site at Bath, Avon, was dedicated to Sul, the Goddess of the Eye of the Sun, whom the Romans conflated with Minerva when they built a vast temple complex over the original site. The healing properties of these waters have brought generations of people to take the waters or bathe in them, and although public access to the curative waters was discontinued in the last seventeen years, it is hoped that they will once more be opened in the near future.

OCTOBER
10

ETAIN, DAUGHTER OF AILILL was given in marriage to the god Midir. However, Midir's first wife, Fuamnach, enchanted Etain into a pool of water, which bred a worm, which turned into a red fly. In this shape, Etain was blown about the winds of the world while Midir sought for her. Oengus mac Og gave her shelter, but she was eventually blown into the cup of an Ulster-woman who swallowed her down and conceived the soul of Etain as a child in her womb. Etain the second grew up in ignorance of her former incarnation and was married to King Eochaid Airem, which is where Midir discovered her. He challenged Eochaid to a game of fidchell in order to win a kiss from Etain, but when he came to claim his kiss, he seized her and flew vertically out of Eochaid's hall back to the domain of faery.

OCTOBER
11

AN IRISH RIDDLE ASKS, 'what son is it that has not been born and will never be born, and yet is named a son?' The answer is 'mac alla' or 'son of a cliff', which is Gaelic for 'an echo'.

OCTOBER
12

THE CONSTELLATION of the Great Bear, Ursa Minor, is called in Gaelic the Drag-bhoth or Fiery House, which may be a kenning for a cauldron. This is strengthened if we look to the name of the Polestar which is called the Star of Knowledge, emblematic of the drops of inspiration which spring from the cauldrons of Celtic tradition.

OCTOBER
13

THE WEARING OF A BELT which offers magical protection appears in Celtic legend. Cormac mac Art's father-in-law, the druid Olc Aiche, appears as a well-appointed herdsman who guards Cormac with five protective girdles against slaying by drowning, fire, sorcery, wolves and evil.

OCTOBER
14

THREE THINGS which are covered in a court: a mead vat, a sentence (judgement) and a song before they are presented before the king.

OCTOBER
15

CAULDRONS ARE THE MAJOR FEATURE of many Celtic stories. They figure as objects of quest, like the Cauldron of Annwn which grants its food only to worthy warriors, or the Cauldron of Rebirth into which dead men can be put and revived, or the Cauldron of Knowledge which confers all wisdom. Many cauldrons are said to emerge from lakes in legend, and archaeology bears out the fact that many votive cauldrons have been found deposited in lakes as part of ritual or funerary customs. Three cauldrons of inspiration are said to reside within the body according to an Irish poetic text, the position of which is reflected by each person's vitality, emotional responsiveness and intellectual capacity. (C & J MATTHEWS 1994)

119

THE HOUSEHOLD FIRE was maintained with skill and blessing by the woman of the house. This Scots Gaelic blessing is said at the smooring or banking in of the fire at night:

I smoor the hearth,
As Mary smoors it;
The vigilance of Brighid and Mary
Be upon the fire and upon the floor
And over the whole household.

Who stands on the grass outside?
Sun-bright Mary and her Son,
The mouth of God requested,
the angel of God spoke;
Angels of promise guard the hearth
Until bright day visits the fire.

LLEU LLAW GYFFES was the son of Arianrhod and an unknown father. His sudden birth at the court of Caer Dathyl was brought about when Arianrhod underwent an examination as an applicant for the position of virgin foot-holder. She stepped over Math's druidic wand and gave birth to Dylan, while Gwydion snatched up the afterbirth and incubated it to create Lleu. Gwydion applied to Arianrhod for a name, arms and a wife for Lleu, none of which Arianrhod would grant. Eventually, he tricked her into giving the first two, but she swore that Lleu would never have a wife of human stock. Gwydion and Math then created Blodeuwedd from flower-essences and married her to Lleu. She betrayed him to her lover, Gronw, who attempted to slay Lleu with a spear, but Lleu took the form of an eagle. Gwydion found and healed Lleu; punished Blodeuwedd by turning her into an owl and aided Lleu to have his revenge on Gronw by returning the spear-throw. Lleu has overlaps with the Irish god Lugh, but the common nature of the two is obscured by the variance of Welsh and Irish traditions.

IN THE IRISH TREE ALPHABET, the letter STR is represented by straif or black thorn.

A SCOTS GAELIC STORY tells how the Faery Queen sent an invitation to all women to receive wisdom from her. Curiosity brought women of all kinds and ages, but few of them believed that the Cup of Mary which the Faery Queen offered them could possibly enlighten them. To the women who remained and wished for wisdom in the inmost hearts, she gave draught after draught until the cup was empty.

THIS RISQUÉ POEM of David O Bruadair is addressed to a bride on her wedding night; the reference to Cuchulainn's spear killing his own son, Connlaech, is the only fatality discussed in this preparation for the assaults of love:

Hardship unfamiliar should
she then discover,
Not yet by her encountered;
Let her not by coldness,
in doing and enduring,
Try to shun her trouble.

Many other vallies, likewise,
have been plundered,
Wounding unforbidden.
To strike across that frontier
is no cause for scrule,
Plentiful its profits.

The exploit of Cú Cuchulainn
with his gapped spear, famous
For its feats of frenzy,
Leaveth in this country
no trace of fatal wounding,
Since the fall of Connlaech.

It left a weighty burthen of
certain magic virtues,
After he was wounded;
Hence it is at present of the pain it causeth
The pleasantest physician.

MERCIER

CERIDWEN IS THE BRITISH GODDESS of Inspiration. It is she who prepares a cauldron of knowledge, culled from the ingredients of every element and season, to compensate her ugly son, Afagddu by giving him great knowledge in place of ugliness. She sets the boy Gwion to tend the cauldron, but he receives the knowledge intended for Afagddu by sucking up the liquor that splashes onto his hand. Gwion escapes from Ceridwen's rage by turning into a hare, a fish , a bird and a grain of wheat, but Ceridwen follows as greyhound, an otter, a hawk and red hen who swallows the grain, conceiving Gwion as her child. She gives birth to him and places him in a leather bag, giving him to the waters on May-Eve. Ceridwen, along with Arianrhod, appears frequently in the poems of Taliesin as the Mistress of Awen (Inspiration) and of druidic initiation.

THE NATURE of the celtic otherworld is conveyed in the image of an apple tree which has a bird in its branches and a pig rooting about beneath it. This image appears in the poems attributed to Myrddin in his madness, and in the *Voyage of Maelduin*. The bird is the messenger of the soul which can travel through the Celtic over-sea world, the pig is the messenger or shape of the soul through the Celtic underworld, and the apple tree distributes the fruit which feeds both body and soul.

OCTOBER
23

THREE OF THE HIGHEST SPIRITS: a student having read his Psalms, a servant having laid down his load, a girl having been made a woman.

OCTOBER
24

THE IRISH BOOK OF RIGHTS laid down the pattern of the Celtic king's week: Sunday for drinking ale, Monday for legal business, Tuesday for chess, Wednesday for greyhound hunting, Thursday for marital intercourse, Friday for horse-racing, Saturday for judgements. (BYRNE)

OCTOBER
25

THE BATTLE OF CAMLANN (542) at which Arthur was mortally wounded by Medraut (Mordred) was an event that became a by-word in the Welsh language for futility. Locations as disparate as Camboglanna, Birdoswald on Hadrian's Wall to Camel in Cornwall have been claimed as the spot at which it took place. Only seven survivors remained alive, such was the slaughter: Sandde Angel's form because of his beauty, Morfran ap Tegid (Afagddu) because of his ugliness, St Cynfelyn from the speed of his horse, St Cedwyn from the world's blessing, St Pedrog from the strength of his spear, Derfel the Strong from his strength, Geneid the Tall from his speed. The tradition of seven survivors echoes Arthur's earlier expedition to realms of Annwn to steal the cauldron; again only seven returned.

OCTOBER
26

THE IRISH GODDESS Macha came from the otherworld to marry Crunniuc mac Agnomain on condition that he should not mention her to others. On hearing the King of Ulster boast about the speed of his horses, Crunniuc boasted that his wife could outrun them, so extraordinary were her powers. Although Macha was heavily pregnant, she was forced to race against the horses, beating them, but falling into labour at the winning post. The circuit of the race became the demarcation of Emain Macha, modern Armagh. As she died giving birth to twins, Macha cursed the Ulstermen with the noinend or nine-fold curse by which they would suffer the pains of childbirth for five days and four nights for nine times nine generations when they were in their utmost need. Only women and boys were exempt from this curse, and, later on, only Cuchulainn who defended Ulster single-handedly during the Cattle Raid of Cooley. To Macha is attributed the building of the first hospital in Ireland.

27

THREE THINGS which preserve remembrance and which stand in the place of witnesses for a person as to his right to land: the place of an old kiln, a stone fireback and a horse-block.

28

IN THE IRISH TREE ALPHABET, the letter R is represented by ruis or elder.

29

GWYDION WAS THE NEPHEW of Math, whose wisdom he lacked, but whose druidic knowledge he shared. It is he that causes war between Dyfed and Gwynedd so that Math leaves his court and the peaceful company of his virgin footholder, Goewin, thus enabling his brother, Gilfaethwy to rape her. His punishment for this deed is to be turned into a stag, a pig and a wolf for a year at a time. He causes Arianrhod's after-birth to be transformed into a living child, his nephew Lleu, whom he protects and promotes; but this leads to a chain of terrible events, including the creation of a woman from flowers, the wounding of Lleu and the loss of all hope.

30

THE DIVINE HERDSMAN is an important figure in Celtic myth, who appears all over the Celtic world in local forms. He appears as an initiatory figure or threshold guardian in many myths. He is called Custennin in the story of Culhwch and Olwen, where he has the role of foster-father to Olwen: here his appearance is fearsomely titanic. In Ireland, the Dagda frequently appears as a rustic, club-carrying herdsman, the trail of whose club creates a magical barrier. The druid Olc Aiche, appears as a well-appointed herdsman who magically protects his son-in-law, Cormac, against death. The Divine Herdsman seems to be a figure who presides over the otherworldly feast, and is a frequent mortal disguise for the gods who visit the realms of humankind.

THE MORRIGHAN is the Irish Goddess of renewal: although she is more frequently called a Goddess of Battle, her role is more subtle than this. The Morrighan is a triple-aspected goddess, comprising Nemhain, Badbh and Macha. She often appears as a crow over battlefields scavenging the slain. The severed head of the Munster warrior, Fothad Canainne speaks of her thus:

About us on this field are
  the bloody horrors of battle;
unspeakable are the guts that
  the Morrigan is washing.
She has descended on as a gloomy guest,
  hurling us into the fray.
She washes her many spoils,
  laughing her dreadful twisted laughter.
She has thrown back her mane;
  the heart in my former shape hates her.

TRANS. CM

However, she is also concerned with sexuality and fertility. She meets with the Dagda on Samhain eve and mates with him at the ford. Their meeting marks the coming together of the great formative powers of the Celtic world, since the end of the summer half of the year also marks the ending of the campaign season: when the Morrighan comes to mate with the Dagda, she lays aside her warring side and with the Father of the Gods, prepares the land for the germination and preparation of winter.

The Morrighan is associated with the Sheela na Gig, a common figure found carved, usually over the Western entrance to churches. She is usually shown as a hag with a gaping, mocking or smiling face, and with both hands opening her distended vulva. The Sheela represents the womb and tomb of life, the essential threshold between the worlds.

Now the doors between the worlds are open once again as we gather to celebrate Samhain, the end of summer, and to welcome the ancestral wisdom once again in the embrace of winter.

BIBLIOGRAPHY

Unless otherwise stated, place of publication is London.

BARBER, Chris *Mysterious Wales* Granada, 1983

BETTEN, Francis S. *St Boniface & St Virgil* St Anselm's Priory, Washington D.C., 1927.

BLATHMAC *Poems* trans. J. Carney, Dublin, Irish Texts Society, 1964

BORD, Janet & Colin *Sacred Waters* Granada, 1985

BUCHAN, David *Scottish Tradition* Routledge & Kegan Paul, 1984

BYRNE, Francis J. *Irish Kings and High Kings* Batsford, 1973

CARMICHAEL, Alexander *Carmina Gadelica* Edinburgh, Floris Books, 1993

CHADWICK, Nora *The Druids* Cardiff, University of Wales Press, 1966

CHRISTIAN, Roy *Well-Dressing in Derbyshire* Derby, Derbyshire Countryside Ltd., 1991

DANAHER, Kevin *The Year in Ireland* Dublin, Mercier Press, 1972

DILLON, Miles *The Cycles of the Kings* Geoffrey Cumberlege, 1946

ELLIS, Peter Berrisford *The Druids* Constable, 1994

FINLAY, Ian *Columba* Glasgow, Richard Drew Publishing, 1990

FLANAGAN, Laurence *A Chronicle of Irish Saints* Belfast, Blackstaff Press, 1990

GEOFFREY OF MONMOUTH *The History of the Kings of Britain* Harmondsworth, Penguin, 1966

GREEN, Miranda *Dictionary of Celtic Myth & Legend* Thames & Hudson, 1992

GREENE, David & O'CONNOR, Frank *A Golden Treasury of Irish Poetry* Macmillan, 1967

HENKEN, Elissa R. *Traditions of the Welsh Saints* Cambridge, D.S. Brewer, 1987

JONES, Noragh *Power of Raven* Edinburgh, Florish Books, 1994

KIGHTLY, Charles *The Customs and Ceremonies of Britain*, Thames & Hudson, 1986

MacLEOD, Fiona *The Divine Adventure* W. Heineman, 1927

MacNEILL, F. M. *The Silver Bough* (3 vols) Glasgow, William McClellan, 1961

MACNEILL, Maire *The Festival of Lughnasadh* Oxford, Oxford University Press, 1962

MATTHEWS, Caitlín *The Celtic Book of the Dead* Aquarian, 1992

MATTHEWS, Caitlín *The Celtic Tradition* Shaftesbury, Element Books, 1995

MATTHEWS, Caitlín *The Little Book of Celtic Blessings* Shaftesbury, Element, 1994

MATTHEWS, Caitlín *Mabon and the Mysteries of Britain* Arkana, 1987

MATTHEWS, Caitlín & John *The Encyclopedia of Celtic Wisdom* Shaftesbury, Element, 1994

MATTHEWS, Caitlín & John *Ladies of the Lake* Aquarian, 1992

MATTHEWS, John *Gawain, Knight of the Goddess* Aquarian, 1990

MATTHEWS, John & Caitlín *Aquarian Guide to British & Irish Mythology* Aquarian Press, 1988

MATTHEWS, John & Caitlín *The Faery Tale Reader* Aquarian Press, 1993

MERCIER, Vivian, *The Irish Comic Tradition* Oxford, Clarendon Press, 1962

MEYER, Kuno *Ancient Irish Poetry* Constable, 1913

MILNER, J. Edward *The Tree Book* Collins & Brown, 1992

MONTGOMERIE, N. & W. *Scottish Nursery Rhymes* Hogarth Press, 1964

MORRIS, John *The Age of Arthur* Weidenfeld and Nicholson, 1973

NAGY, Joseph F. *The Wisdom of the Outlaw* Berkeley, University of California Press, 1985

NENNIUS *British History and the Welsh Annals* Phillimore & Co, 1980

O CATHASAIGH, Tomás *The Heroic Biography of Cormac Mac Airt* Dublin, Dublin Institute for Advanced Studies, 1977

O'FIACH, Tomás *Columbanus* Dublin, Veritas, 1974

O'MALLEY, Brian *A Pilgrim's Manual* Marlborough, Paulinus Press, 1985

Oxford Companion to the Literature of Wales ed. Meic Stephens, Oxford, Oxford University Press, 1986

Oxford Dictionary of Saints ed. David H. Farmer, Oxford, Oxford University Press, 1978

PLUTARCH *Moralia, vol. 12* trans. Harold Cherniss, W. Heinemann Ltd., 1958

REES, Alwyn & Brinley *Celtic Heritage* Thames & Hudson, 1961

RICHARDS, Melville *The Laws of Hywel Dda* Liverpool, Liverpool Univ. Press, 1954

RIMMER, *Joan The Irish Harp* Cork, Mercier Press, 1969

ROSS, Ann *Pagan Celtic Britain* Cardinal, 1974

SELLNER, Edward C. *Wisdom of the Celtic Saints* Notre Dame Indiana, Ave Maria Press, 1993

SHAW, Margaret Fay *Folksongs and Folklore of South Uist* Routledge & Kegan Paul, 1955

SIMPSON, Jacqueline *The Folklore of the Welsh Border* B.T. Batsford, 1976

SKENE, William F. *The Four Ancient Books of Wales* Edinburgh, Edmonston & Douglas, 1868

TOULSON, Shirley *The Celtic Year* Shaftesbury, Element, 1993

TOWILL, E.S. *The Saints of Scotland* Edinburgh, St Andrews Press, 1978

TREVELYAN, Marie *Folk Lore and Folk Stories of Wales* Eilliot Stock, 1909

Trioedd Ynys Prydein ed. Rachel Bromwich, Cardiff, University of Wales Press, 1961

INDEX

Macha - 26 Oct
Maelduin - 27 Jun
Manannan - 6 Apr, 1 Jun
Marianus Scotus - 22 Dec
martyrdoms - 27 May
Mary the Virgin - 25 Mar,
 15 Aug
Math ap Mathonwy -
 6 Dec, 14 Feb, 26 Feb
Medb - 15 Jul
memory - 11 Dec
Merlin/Myrddin - 4 Jan,
 10 Aug, 17 Aug
Modron - 26 Mar, 9 Apr
Mog Ruith - 24 Jun
Mon - 9 Mar
Mongan - 3 Jul
Morgen - 16 Mar
Morrighan - 27 Feb,
 28 Jun, 31 Oct
Mothers - 3 May
mumming - 29 Dec
music - 9 Jul
musical branch - 1 Jun,
 19 Jun

N

Nechtan - 9 Jan
Nehelenia - 11 Apr
Nemetona - 19 Mar
night - 7 Nov
Nodens - 28 Jan
Noson lawen - 3 Jan
Nuadu - 28 Jan
number - 8 Nov, 8 Dec,
 7 Jan, 8 Aug, 8 Sep, 17 Sep,
 19 Sep, 8 Oct

O

oaths - 18 Aug
Oengus Og - 1 Jul, 10 Oct
ogham alphabet - 24 Nov,
 12 Dec, 30 Dec, 10 Jan, 21
 Jan, 4 Feb, 22 Feb,
 28 Feb, 10 Mar, 3 Apr, 12
 May, 17 May, 10 Jun, 11 Jul,
 25 Jul, 22 Aug,
 7 Sep, 7 Oct, 18 Oct,
 28 Oct

Ogma - 21 Jul
ordeals - 19 Apr
otherworld - 22 Oct

P

Padstow - 20 May
Pelagius - 6 Jul
Picts - 13 Mar
pillar stones - 24 Mar
prayers - 15 Feb, 20 Feb,
 15 Mar, 31 Mar, 22 Jul
prophecy & divination -
 16 Dec, 19 Jul, 26 Aug, 26
 Sep, 1 Oct
Pryderi - 29 Nov
Pwyll - 4 Oct

R

regions of Ireland - 23 Dec,
 22 Mar, 22 Jun, 23 Jun, 22
 Sep
Rhiannon - 4 Sep
riddles - 21 Feb, 29 Aug,
 6 Oct, 11 Oct
Roquepertuse - 12 Nov

S

St Adamnan - 23 Sep
St Aidan - 31 Aug
St Beuno - 3 Nov, 21 Apr
St Brendan - 16 May
St Brigit - 1 Feb, 2 Feb,
 29 Feb
St Canair - 28 Nov
St Ciaran of Saighir - 5 Mar
St Collen - 21 May
St Columba - 9 Jun, 10 Sep
St Columbanus - 21 Nov
St Cuthbert - 20 Mar
St David - 1 Mar
St Dwynwen - 25 Jan
St Finnian - 10 Sep
St Gobhnat - 11 Feb
St Gwenfrewi
 (Winefride) - 3 Nov
St Hilda - 18 Nov
St Illtud - 6 Nov
St Ita - 15 Jan
St Kentigern - 14 Jan

St Kevin - 3 Jun
St Madrun - 9 Apr
St Maelruain - 7 Jul
St Maelrubha - 25 Aug
St Martin - 11 Nov
St Melangell - 2 Dec
St Moling - 17 Jun
St Moluag - 25 Jun
St Ninian - 16 Sep
St Non - 3 Mar
St Oengus - 11 Mar
St Padarn - 15 Apr
St Patrick - 17 Mar, 12 Jul,
 26 Jul
St Samson - 28 Jul
St Samthann - 19 Dec
St Ursinus - 20 Dec
St Virgil - 27 Nov
Samhain - 1 Nov
satires - 20 Aug
Scathach - 14 Nov
seasonal poems - 23 Nov,
 7 Dec
Sedulius Scotus - 10 Apr
Sheela na Gig - 31 Oct
songs - 25 Dec, 6 Jan,
 3 Feb, 31 May, 3 Oct
soul - 12 Apr,
soul-cakes - 2 Nov
sovereignty - 6 Aug,
 23 Aug, 25 Sep, 24 Oct
stars - 10 Dec, 2 Jan, 22 May,
 21 Jul, 22 Jul, 12 Oct
Suibhne - 6 Sep
sun - 2 Apr, 13 Apr

T

Taliesin - 17 Feb, 30 Apr
tarbh feis - 19 Jan
Three Hooded Ones -
 25 Nov
Tlachtga - 16 Nov
tree lore - 29 May
triads - 5 Nov, 5 Dec, 5 Jan,
 27 Jan, 5 Feb, 16 Feb,
 4 Mar, 5 Apr, 14 Apr,
 18 Apr, 5 May, 5 Jun,
 18 Jun, 5 Jul, 17 Jul, |
 23 Jul, 5 Aug, 12 Aug, 19 Aug,

 24 Aug, 30 Aug, 5 Sep, 12
 Sep, 24 Sep,
 2 Oct, 5 Oct, 23 Oct,
 27 Oct
Tuan mac Carill - 7 Mar
tuathal - 4 Nov
Twrch Trwyth - 24 Jan

W

weather lore - 1 Feb,
 12 Feb, 2 Mar, 29 Jun,
 6 Aug
wells & springs - 9 Dec,
 9 Feb, 4 Jun, 14 Jul,
 9 Oct
wren - 26 Dec

Acknowledgements

Birmingham Museum
and Art Gallery:
A.F. Sandys, *Morgan Le Fey 29*
Sir E. Burne Jones, *The Failure of
Sir Gawaine 70*
A.J. Gaskin *Kilhwch, The King's
Son 98*

Cameron Collection: *21, 23, 36,
48, 52, 59, 86, 89,99, 120, 121*

Glasgow Museum and Art
Gallery: Sir Noel Paton, *The Fairy
Raid* (details) *12, 17*

Miranda Green *60L*

King Arthur's Great Halls, *26L, 49*

Laing Art Gallery, Newcastle
upon Tyne: John Martin,
The Bard 104

Stuart Littlejohn *47*

Michael Macliamoir *63, 78, 85, 87,
103, 107*

National Galleries of Scotland:
J. Duncan, *St Bride 40*, (detail) *90*

Chesca Potter *19, 24, 25M, 94, 116,
124*

St Andrews Chapel, Fort
Augustus Abbey: photo, Giles
Conacher OSB, Pluscarden
Abbey *32,33*